GETTING CONTROL OF YOUR ANGER

A Clinically Proven, Three-Step Plan
for Getting to the Root of the
Problem and Resolving It

ROBERT ALLAN, PH.D.

WITH DONNA BLASS

McGraw·Hill

New York   Chicago   San Francisco   Lisbon   London   Madrid   Mexico City
Milan   New Delhi   San Juan   Seoul   Singapore   Sydney   Toronto

The McGraw·Hill Companies

Library of Congress Cataloging-in-Publication Data

Allan, Robert, 1945–
    Getting control of your anger : a clinically proven, 3-step plan for getting to the root of the problem and solving it / Robert Allan with Donna Blass ; produced by the Philip Lief Group.
        p.   cm.
    Includes bibliographical references.
    ISBN 0-07-144884-5 (alk. paper)
    1. Anger.   I. Blass, Donna.   II. Philip Lief Group.   III. Title.

BF575.A5A45   2006
152.4'7—dc22   2005022614

1 2 3 4 5 6 7 8 9 0 FGR/FGR 0 9 8 7 6 5

ISBN 0-07-144884-5

McGraw-Hill books are available at special quantity discounts to use as premiums and sales promotions, or for use in corporate training programs. For more information, please write to the Director of Special Sales, Professional Publishing, McGraw-Hill, Two Penn Plaza, New York, NY 10121-2298. Or contact your local bookstore.

The anecdotes contained in this book have been created as a didactic tool. While some accurately describe actual case histories, most have been formed by combining aspects of several different cases and life experiences in the author's and writer's lives in order to highlight particular points in the text.

This book is printed on acid-free paper.

This book is dedicated to two of the most important influences in my life: my father, Bernard, and my mentor, Meyer Friedman, M.D. You both taught me a great deal—however, not always in the way you hoped.

Contents

Acknowledgments

First and foremost, this book owes a great debt of gratitude to Dr. Lynda H. Powell for her brilliant idea of the "hook." This remarkably powerful metaphor has helped transform my own anger and my life. In addition, the hook has immeasurably improved the lives of my family, patients, colleagues, and acquaintances—virtually anyone who has come in contact with the idea. We have all benefited a great deal from Dr. Powell's strategy to help reclaim our impulses and maintain our freedom to choose, rather than become a slave to our initial impulses. The hook forms the nucleus for the anger management program contained in this book. In short, this book could not exist without Dr. Powell's metaphor.

I am also greatly indebted to Judy Linden, who approached me with the idea of writing a book about angry parents, angry children, and breaking the cycle.

Judy found a new job midway through the preparation of this book; however, she must be credited for developing the idea for a book about anger in families. She has also been a very good friend and mentor, even after her departure. Thank you, Judy, and thanks also to Karina Davidson, Ph.D., for recommending me to her.

My writer, Donna Blass, has greatly helped to bring my formal, academic prose to life; she has also made substantial contributions to the content of the book and I am truly appreciative. I would also like to thank my second editor at The Philip Lief Group, Judy Capodanno, for picking up the ball after Judy Linden's departure. She put up with my struggle with theoretical issues and helped to get my points across clearly; she also dealt with the difficulties inherent in deciding what material to include in the final version of the text.

My patients have taught me a great deal, and I am very grateful for their trust and confidence. I hope they will all be shocked by the opening sentence of this book, insisting, "Oh no, not Dr. Allan—he's too kind to have an anger problem like that."

Many others have helped with the development of the anger management program contained in this book, as well as the opportunity to practice and develop my skills as a psychologist and psychotherapist. From the Division of Psychiatry at New York

Presbyterian Hospital–Weill Medical College of Cornell University, I would like to thank Jack Barchas, M.D.; Philip Wilner, M.D.; Susan Evans, Ph.D.; Baruch Fishman, Ph.D.; Robert Millman, M.D.; and George Makari, M.D. I am particularly grateful to Robert Michels, M.D.; Ngaere Baxter, Ph.D.; and Martin V. Cohen, Ph.D., for their comments on earlier versions of Chapter 2. David Wolitzky, Ph.D., and Robert R. Holt, Ph.D., former professors at New York University, where I obtained my Ph.D. in clinical psychology many years ago, provided helpful comments for my section on Freud and psychoanalysis.

At Cornell in the division of cardiology, I would like to extend my gratitude to Stephen Scheidt, M.D.; Jeffrey Fisher, M.D.; and Paul Kligfield, M.D. Beverly Borg and Samuel Mann, M.D., always provide ongoing friendship and encouragement. At the New York Presbyterian Hospital Cardiac Health Center, I thank Abby Jacobson, R.N.; Gerardo Zullo, M.D.; Mary Smith, R.N.; and Andrew Chai, Tina Caballes, and Evelyn Felstein for their continuing support. At the New York Hospital of Queens Cardiac Health Center, John Nicholson, M.D.; Donna Cheslik, R.N., M.A.; Gerri Donlon, R.N.; Florito Bacani, R.N.; exercise physiologists Jamie Foster and Kiseok Lee. Kathleen Ryan and Barbara Taylor always have a friendly hello.

At the Board of Cooperative Educational Services in Rockland County, thank you to Dr. Eileen McCarthy; Paul Citerella; Barry Fitzgerald, Ph.D.; Mary Sitgraves, Ph.D.; Norman Stein, Ph.D.; and Jeffrey Goidel, Ph.D. At Stony Point Elementary School, I would like to thank Principal Diane Banes, Elizabeth Scaccio, Joyce Rothstein, Geanne Hernandez, Maureen Gowan, and the teachers and parents who taught me about their anger management concerns from their questions and comments during my anger management seminars.

My wife, Amanda, and daughter, Sara, continue to help with my ongoing anger management issues, as do my good friends Herb and Karen Friedman. My office mate, Michael DeMeo, M.D., provides ongoing, much appreciated doses of optimism. I am eternally grateful to my late father, who had a difficult life and provided the basis for much of my understanding of anger, as well as the motivation to help myself and others learn how to better manage this sometimes destructive emotion. I thank my mother for her unconditional support throughout my life. And my mother-in-law, Millicent Matland, for her helpful comments on the manuscript.

Introduction

"You sound cruel," said my therapy supervisor as we listened to the tape from one of my very first cases. I couldn't disagree. My voice sounded caustic and I was crushed. Drawn to psychology in part to overcome an emotionally abusive childhood, I had always been afraid of my father's anger, which could erupt without warning at any instant. Once when I was around ten, he hit his thumb with a hammer and exploded with an expletive so forceful that I felt catapulted off the ground by the power of his rage. And yet, here I was in graduate school, after several years of my own therapy, sounding like a subdued—but nonetheless cruel—version of him.

My father's rage had also terrified my mother and sister, since the threat of abandonment was always in the air. My mother, who had limited marketable skills, never risked talking back to her husband, whom she feared might leave us desolate—just as her younger sister's husband had done to his family. My, what she put up with over those years! My father would explode in rage whenever he didn't get his way, and it wasn't always possible to know in advance just what was "his way." One night after a business triumph, he was so taken with himself that he threw his dinner across the dining room into the living room, insisting that he wanted to eat steak every night. After such explosions, there was a deadly silence in the house that lasted for days, until a gradual thaw arrived with the same unpredictability as the outbursts.

Yet there I was in my midtwenties, a budding clinical psychologist with a scathing voice. What was I to do? I continued in my therapy. I also became a "free spirit" embracing "free love," the zeitgeist of the time, in denial of my own anger. However, a succession of girlfriends left me, complaining that I was mean. I had great difficulty believing them. One of the conundrums about one's own anger is that it's so easy to rationalize and blame on someone else: if only you hadn't done such and such, I wouldn't be angry.

My father's anger inadvertently led me to the world of cardiology. He had his first heart attack at the age of forty-six, and I hoped to avoid a similar fate. In 1981, I made the first of many visits to San Francisco, where I met Dr. Meyer Friedman, a cardiologist and co-originator of "type A behavior." Dr. Friedman's research provided some of the first scientific data linking coronary heart disease and stress. At the Meyer Friedman Institute, I soon learned that "free-floating," or easily aroused, hostility is one of the two cardinal symptoms of type A behavior (the other is "time pressure"—doing too much in too little time). Some people can transform nearly any stressful situation into an opportunity to vent their anger.

The term *stress* generally refers to conditions that take place outside of us. How we react to major stressors like the loss of a job or loved one, as well as more common and frequent stressors such as disagreements with the children, becomes a central part of our personal psychology. In other words, some people—myself included—characteristically respond to externally stressful conditions with anger. Indeed, I often notice an angry internal monologue playing in my thoughts whenever conditions are not as I want.

In the course of both my therapy practice and my life, I discovered that I was far from alone in my anger problems. When frustrated, many of us are apt to express our feelings with vigor. Indeed, psychologists and psychiatrists have long suspected that *not* expressing emotions can lead to illness. It was Dr. Friedman's pioneering discovery that the physiological consequences of repeatedly "blowing one's top" (in other words, expressing one's anger) were implicated in triggering heart attacks—just the opposite of what I had learned in psychology. In other words, the damage to our arteries and our hearts comes not just from the external stressors in our lives, but how we repeatedly react to those stressors. While we may feel invigorated when we "blow off steam," the adrenaline rush acts very much like an illicit drug: it may make us feel good in the moment, but with repeated use it ultimately damages our health. One core issue I will discuss at length is whether it is best to express anger spontaneously, the moment you feel it. For now, the answer is a resounding *no*.

This book is the culmination of my decades-long study of anger. More than a simple distillation of what has been written about anger in psychology and philosophy, this book explores the origins, nature, and effects of anger in the family. Anger is very often a family affair. As the aphorism says, "The apple doesn't fall far from the tree."

My father was my teacher in ways that were far from what he hoped. One of the first things that I learned in psychology—and was able to confirm by empirical research—is that much of our behavior is learned by imitation. Social skills develop early in life, patterned after what one observes. So while I was always contemptuous of my father's rage and knew of its painful effects firsthand, I was unfortunately doomed to follow in his footsteps—patterning my own behavior after his without even realizing it. However, I hated my father's anger and vowed that I would never become a terrifying ogre like him. Instead, I would become a psychologist.

During my years at what was once the New York Hospital–Cornell Medical Center, and is now known as New York Presbyterian Hospital–Weill Medical College of Cornell University, I began working with people—young and old—to find ways of better managing their stress and anger. In 1984, with respected cardiologist Dr. Stephen Scheidt, I cofounded the Coronary Risk Reduction Program, a secondary prevention program for those who already have heart disease. The program was heavily based on new anger management techniques that were evolving in my work.

Within months, I was struck by a similarity among my diverse group of patients. Like me, many had parents who suffered from heart disease. Moreover, because the program focused on modifying negative behaviors, many also voiced considerable concern about their constant anger, remembering a parent's, and even a grandparent's, anger. Anger seemed to play a part in every aspect of their lives, affecting not only their physical condition but also their relationships with family members of different generations. I was repeatedly asked, "Are my children learning to respond to stress with anger?" "Will they, too, succumb to heart disease in later life?" "Are we all stuck in a vicious cycle prompted by anger?"

In addition to my appointment at New York Presbyterian–Weill Cornell, I have also maintained a parttime position as a clinical psychologist in a special education school setting where I work with troubled children and adolescents—many of whom have great difficulty controlling their anger. In the adolescent population, anger sometimes leads to violence. Once expressed, anger is often difficult to contain, particularly when it involves other individuals who are also prone to physical confrontation. Again, my young students expressed deep concern: "I'm just like my father . . . my mother . . . my brother. Am I doomed?" For me, a pattern began to emerge that set the stage for the focus of this book.

The damaging effects of excessive anger are only too apparent. In my own life, as well as in the lives of my patients, I have seen the enormous benefits of learning how to manage anger more effectively. What this means in most circumstances is *not* expressing anger in the moment, but waiting until later on when you have cooled down. My all-time favorite quote about anger comes from the sixteenth-century French essayist and philosopher Montaigne, who said, "There is no passion that so shakes the clarity of our judgment as anger. Things truly seem different to us once we have quieted and cooled down." Here you will find my clinically proven system for managing anger, the essence of which can be reduced to three steps:

1. Identify the "hook" that lures your anger. Don't "bite the hook"; don't express your anger.
2. Identify the "need" that is causing your anger. There are two generally unrecognized psychological needs that fuel anger: one is the need for respect, the other involves a breach of territory. I'll explain how to determine which need is fueling your rage.
3. Fill the need.

As you will learn later on, identifying unfulfilled needs that cause anger requires a little education. We are often angry for reasons of which we are unaware. In the meantime, whenever you find yourself feeling angry, ask yourself, *What is my goal? How can I obtain a desired outcome?* or even *What do I want?*

As you go through this program, keep in mind that you don't have to psychoanalyze your past to manage your anger. That will get you nowhere. However, you cannot see yourself as a victim, either. While there will always be good reasons to become angry, the anger is exclusively ours. In order to manage our anger, we have to "own it." Blaming it on someone else or responding with a put-down only delays the process of managing anger effectively. While it may feel like a little "victory" in the short term to put someone down, relationships are often damaged. At some level, the angry individual knows that his or her anger has contributed to a damaged relationship.

Anger management has helped my patients' families feel better, too—better about the quality of their time together and more loving toward their formerly angry partner or parent. Being around an angry person is no fun. As I can attest to firsthand, my father's explosive rage kept us on edge all the time. My mother, sister, and I were always fearful that we might bear the brunt of my father's rage. This could be terrifying, especially when my sister and I were younger, and particularly when his rage was accompanied by verbal abuse and the threat of abandonment. Rage-filled families are unhappy families.

Finally, this book provides insight in how to break the cycle of angry fathers and angry sons, angry mothers and angry daughters. For the most part, it is up to the parents to break the cycle. Children can succeed only so far in managing their anger if their parents, their role models, are always "blowing their tops." Who can children pattern their behavior after, if not the people they look up to? The first critical step to successful anger management is to avoid giving in to the impulse to express your anger. While it may seem unnatural at first, you will soon discover what Montaigne noted: things do seem different to us once we have quieted and cooled down. Not expressing anger when you first feel it increases your options. You can always "let them have it" later on, if after careful consideration you decide that such a course of action may be the most effective. But it rarely is. As the distinguished psychologist Silvan Tomkins said some years ago, directly expressing anger is a way of making a "bad situation worse."

But oh, was I anguished by those three words spoken by my therapy supervisor, "You sound cruel." After more than thirty years, I still feel shame and embarrassment when I acknowledge this incident. In truth, my supervisor only confirmed what I had already known from listening to the tape myself. His validation of my anger set me on a course of correction that has lasted more than thirty years and continues to this day.

What caused my cruelty? I was frustrated. My patient at the time, a person who suffered from borderline personality disorder, ran rings around me. I would ask a question, and she would take the conversation in a completely different direction. But I didn't know that this was the case until it was pointed out by my supervisor. She, the patient, was running the show—not I, her therapist. I felt disrespected but didn't know it!

This has been perhaps my biggest discovery of all: we feel angry when we feel disrespected. But we don't usually realize that the *disrespect* is what's causing our anger: instead, we argue about the details of a difference of opinion, missing the forest for the trees.

It is my hope that my journey into self-awareness and self-imposed anger management will inspire you to gain greater control of your anger. I sincerely hope my words improve your own life, as well as the lives of those around you.

Let's begin.

Part I

The Seeds and Fruits of Anger

The Origins of Anger

Debbie is looking forward to a nice weekend, the first one in a long time when her husband Paul won't be working. She manages to leave her office early, knowing she'll have a few hours to herself before her children get home from school. But Debbie's good mood quickly begins to dissolve as soon as she walks into the house. First, she presses the blinking answering machine to hear a long list of complaints from her mother, including news that Deb's father has neglected (again) to mail in his driver's license renewal form. That means they will need to rely on Deb to drive them to a doctor's appointment the next day. Furious, Debbie thinks, *Why do my parents assume it's my job to drop everything any time* they *mess up or need something done?* She stomps her feet all the way to the kitchen, only to discover that someone has left the milk container out on the counter; surely it has gone sour by now. In the mail, there's news that a collection agency has been alerted about an overdue bill—one Paul said he paid.

Across town, Paul is having his own problems. He gets news that an important report needs to be revised by Monday so that it can be shown to a client. *So there goes his no-work weekend.* And as much as Paul would love to delegate the job to an underling, he's nervous. He made a careless accounting error last month, so he's feeling more insecure than usual. And there is the new guy who is already winning points for his inventive ideas. To make matters worse, Paul knows Debbie will be furious when she finds out he has to work. Well, that's her problem! *She's too damn demanding*, Paul thinks. Funny how she expects him to understand whenever *she* has a schedule conflict.

By the time the children come home from school, Debbie has worked herself up into a fury. "Who left the milk out?" she demands to know. "And why can't you kids ever, ever pick up your clothes? Your rooms are pigsties, and I'm sick of cleaning up after you!" Pigsties or not, the kids decide to retreat to those messy rooms. They've experienced their mother's outbursts before, and they know it's smart to stay out of her way.

By the time Paul gets home, he feels both defensive and defiant. Yes, he's got to work, he tells Debbie, but how does she expect the bills to be paid if he doesn't meet the demands of his job? "Funny you should bring up bills," Debbie sarcastically jabs. "Do you realize we're now in collection because of that electric bill you swore you paid? How could you be such a moron? And now you keep making the same stupid mistakes. Do you have any idea what it's like to deal with someone so incompetent?"

The fight is on; the verbal assaults get worse and the insults get uglier. After struggling hard to contain himself, Paul blurts out, "You're always so damned hysterical! So we'll pay the bill and *nothing*, absolutely nothing will happen to our credit rating, Debbie! Why don't you just shut up? I walk in the door after dealing with really important business matters and difficult people all day and you bust my chops about a bill I forgot to pay. Sometimes I wonder why I bother to come home at all!"

While Debbie and Paul have their screaming match, their children are upstairs, trying to tune out the vicious words of their parents. They've heard it all before . . . and they assume they will hear it again.

If you grew up in an angry family, chances are you, too, have observed scenes like this one. If you are currently living in an angry family, you might be part of these kinds of exchanges on a regular basis. You are probably painfully aware of a gap between the nurturing environment you want to provide for your family and the reality of what is happening in your own home. Maybe you sometimes catch yourself saying the same cruel things to your own son or daughter that a parent said to you. And you may be haunted by questions such as: *Why am I reliving something so painful? Why do I sometimes feel as if I'm reenacting a scene from my own past, and inflicting the same kind of hurt on my children that my parents inflicted on me? Is anger something that just runs in the family, like brown eyes or red hair? Is it genetic? Inherited? Learned? Is there something I can do to put a stop to all this distress and anguish?*

There is good news: anger doesn't have to rule your life or impose undue pain on your children. You can break the cycle by learning how to manage your anger in a more constructive, effective way. But first, it's vital to explore the very nature of anger—and understand why it remains such a frequently misunderstood and poorly managed emotion.

What Is Anger?

At first glance it may seem foolish to even pose the question: *what is anger?* Of course we know the feeling all too well; it ranges from mild annoyance to outright fury, a profound state of emotional discomfort. Who needs it?

Yet, from a strictly biological standpoint, anger is actually a very good thing. Much like pain and fear, it serves as a kind of physiologic warning device—alerting us that something is wrong and needs to be attended to. The pain of a throbbing ankle may indicate a sprain; it warns us to get off our feet to avoid worsening an injury. Imagine how dangerous it would be to touch a hot stove if we did not experience the sensation of pain to quickly force our hand away. The sensation of dread we feel while walking down a deserted street may compel us to quickly seek safer, more populated surroundings. In each case, the discomfort brought on by pain or fear not only makes us aware of a real or potential problem—it prompts us to find a remedy.

Anger works in much the same way. Developmentally, anger is a natural reaction to a failure in *homeostasis*, which can be defined as an organism's tendency to maintain stable biological conditions. Whenever our equilibrium has been thrown off—by some discomfort such as hunger, a light that is too bright, or an overwhelming temperature shift—our physiologic processes automatically adjust to restore a sense of balance. For instance, if you step out from a dark room into sunshine, your pupils instantly contract to let your eyes adjust to the sudden brightness; step into a dark movie theater, and your pupils dilate to let in as much light as possible. If we feel too hot, we perspire, which is the body's way of cooling off the skin; conversely, we shiver in the cold to conserve body heat. These are simple examples of how the body restores equilibrium when physical conditions change, but the system works in much the same way when it comes to our emotions. For instance, we often feel annoyed at physical discomfort, or we feel fear and anger in response to a perceived threat.

Beginning in infancy, human beings are programmed to have their needs met by the surrounding environment. Think of a newborn. His primary goal is to seek comfort: that is, to maximize pleasure and minimize pain. Like every other human, the baby experiences a variety of sensations—positive and negative—that spring from both internal and external sources: A soft blanket, a soothing voice, a full and satisfied belly all signal *Life is good; my needs are being met.* Hunger pangs, a wet diaper, or a hot and stuffy room tell the baby *Whoa, something's wrong here!* And when the baby is hungry or uncomfortable, he seizes on the one tool he's got at his disposal to address the situation: he cries. In fact, that fabled cry is a way of signaling caregivers, a technique to ensure the baby has a "voice" (even before he has the ability to verbalize) to let others know his needs are not being met.

With prolonged discomfort, a baby's cries will gradually grow louder and more insistent; if help doesn't arrive, that cry will eventually turn into a scream, a powerful signal that something is wrong. If you've ever been around a wailing infant, you know how hard it is to ignore a baby's scream. It's a real attention-grabber.

This is one origin of anger. The baby senses he's in a state of distress, and if his needs continue to be frustrated the protest grows louder. These roots of anger in infancy are universal, cutting across all cultures and circumstances. Every infant goes through the inevitable periods of frustration and discomfort that lead to anger.

Let's take a look at what happens when a baby's cries are answered. The infant's sobs attract the atten-

tion of a concerned caregiver—the mother, let's say—
who responds with a soothing word and gentle caress.
Mother senses that the baby needs to be fed, changed,
or held; she takes steps to fix whatever is amiss. (Perhaps the baby is hungry or a window needs to be
adjusted to make the room more comfortable.) From
the baby's vantage, a sense of equilibrium is restored;
his needs have been filled and he experiences a sense
of comfort, of calm. Homeostasis is once more
attained. Babies tend to gurgle and coo when they are
content—a far "cry" from the howling angst of a full-
blown wail.

When Adults Lose Homeostasis

Now fast-forward thirty or forty years. As adults, we
surely have much more influence over life events than
we did as babies; we're able to express our wishes and
exert some control over our environment. So why
should maintaining homeostasis still be a problem?

Picture this scene: you're a parent of two young
children, and you're having a hectic day. Things get
even more harried when you find out that you have to
make an unscheduled trip to pick up your eight-year-
old from an after-school Brownie meeting. No sweat:
after asking a neighbor to watch your four-year-old,
you set out to make the five-mile trip.

But along the way, things start to go awry: an accident has brought traffic to a standstill. You're stuck,

unable to move or navigate an alternate route. As for the "no-sweat" part, a light on the dashboard suddenly comes on, signaling that your car is in danger of overheating. In response, you turn off the air conditioner—and the temperature is a sweltering ninety-five degrees with lots of stifling humidity. Then you discover that, in your quick dash from the house, you forgot to bring along your water bottle and cell phone.

So here is the situation: you're hot, thirsty, unable to move, unable to communicate. You don't know how long you will be trapped in this spot, but you *do* know your daughter is waiting—maybe getting fretful and nervous—and that compounds the stress. You can't get word to anyone about your whereabouts. In short, your most pressing physiologic needs are being frustrated, your homeostasis has been seriously compromised, and you're getting *angry!*

Minutes pass, and eventually the accident is getting cleared away (lots of smashed metal, but no serious injuries). As your car starts to edge along, the "hot" light goes out, and you click on the air conditioner once again for blissful relief. Up ahead, there's a gas station, equipped with a pay phone and a soda machine. After letting your daughter's school know you will be arriving pronto—and alerting your babysitting neighbor you'll be back shortly—you get a cold drink to quench your thirst. So what's happening now on the physiologic level? As circumstances shift, you regain that crucial locus of control, that ability to function and address what's wrong. Your inner equilibrium is restored, your needs have been filled, and your anger gradually dissipates.

Adult Anger: The Biological Underpinnings

You may suspect that anger is more than infantile behavior that is "all grown up"—and you are right. Biologically speaking, that discomfiting sensation of racing heart, sweaty palms, hyperarousal, and a need to defend your turf is closely linked to another of nature's self-protective mechanisms, the fight-or-flight response. Whenever we are faced with a sudden threat to our well-being—whether it's a car hurtling through a red light or stern words like "The boss wants to see you"—our bodies kick into gear. Their mission: mobilize all biological resources and get ready to meet the danger. This is what's known as the fight-or-flight response. From an evolutionary standpoint, fight-or-flight is a holdover from the days when our ancestors faced some very compelling threats, such as a saber-toothed tiger waiting to attack. In such a situation, humans had to—quite literally—make an instant decision about whether it was wiser to stay and fight the enemy or swiftly take flight and head for cover. Accordingly, an area of the brain called the amygdala initiates a sequence of biochemical changes that get the body primed to either fight hard or run fast.

What exactly happens when the fight-or-flight response is activated? Adrenaline and cortisol—the "stress hormones"—are rapidly released into the bloodstream. As a result, our bodies undergo some dramatic changes very quickly to help us perceive and react to a sudden physical challenge. Respiration and heart rate increase. Blood is routed toward the large muscles and limbs (preparing us to move quickly) and away from the stomach and intestines (good digestion is not a top priority when the body is poised to confront danger). Our pupils dilate. Our senses go into a state of high alert: we are likely to have sharper sight, quicker reaction time, and a greater awareness of what is going on around us. At the same time, one sensation becomes diminished—our perception of pain. In the peak of the fight-or-flight response, we are far less likely to feel any kind of physical discomfort. It's as if our bodies are telling us: "There's plenty of time to hurt later; right now, we've got a job to do."

You may have heard some dramatic examples of how people can harness extraordinary strength in the face of danger: the parent who lifts up a car to free trapped children, the accident victim who somehow is able to walk a remarkable distance and find help even when stricken with severe injuries. Perhaps you have even experienced some version of this phenomenon yourself. If so, you know firsthand what the fight-or-flight response feels like: that surge of adrenaline fills us with a rare kind of "animal courage" in moments when we are called on to protect and defend ourselves or our loved ones.

But there is something else that is crucial to understand: by its very nature, the fight-or-flight response is designed to move us quickly into empowerment mode. It can bypass our rational mind, the place where we weigh options and carefully craft solutions. When we're fueled by adrenaline, we are focused on short-term survival, not long-term consequences. Making well-thought-out choices with an awareness of how those choices might impact our lives—or the lives of those we love—is not the priority.

That's one reason we're so prone to doing and saying things in the heat of the moment—in other words, at the height of the fight-or-flight response—that we later regret. Newspaper headlines detail outlandish stories of people "losing it" over such seemingly innocuous matters as someone cutting into a long line or having the wrong meal brought to the table in a restaurant. Far more common are the times we shout first and ask questions later; like Debbie and Paul, we may hurl stinging, abusive accusations at a loved one without giving a thought to how bitter or hurtful our words sound—or what effect they might have.

Another thing to know: in the hyperaroused fight-or-flight state, we are on the lookout for danger and more poised than usual to see everything as a possible threat. Physiologically, this heightened sensitivity is logical, since it keeps us extra-alert (after all, that tiger from which you just escaped may still be lurking nearby!). But practically, there can be some drawbacks. In this particular moment, our fears are exaggerated. We may overreact to the slightest negative remark, even the hint of a dirty look. We have a predisposition to perceive possible threats.

In the face of threat, our prejudices and insecurities are more likely to guide our behavior. Imagine that your car has just been rear-ended by a seventeen-year-old driver. In that frightening moment, every belief you've ever harbored about irresponsible teenagers is likely to come to the forefront. You may be ready to lash out at permissive parents, the irreverent ways teens dress ("All those horrible tattoos and body piercings!"), or the outright rudeness of young people who spend all day hanging around your local convenience store. Only later—when you have calmed down, realized no one was injured, and discovered that your youthful assailant is actually a nice young man who keeps apologizing for his failure to yield—are you able to see the situation from a more accurate perspective. When anger subsides, things look a lot clearer.

Once triggered, how does this fight-or-flight response work itself through to a natural conclusion? After the immediate threat has been confronted, our physical reactions—rapid heartbeat, heightened awareness, insensitivity to pain—gradually begin to abate. Things return to normal. Our minds and bodies have faced the danger and are ready to return to their usual state—but not for a while.

How the Ancient Fight-or-Flight Response Meets Contemporary Challenges

Clearly, the fight-or-flight response is nature's way of getting us primed to fend off bodily harm. And when we face real dangers to our physical safety, the response is invaluable. Yet nearly all of the threats of modern living aren't as immediate or overwhelming as the proverbial saber-toothed tiger. More likely, we're threatened by traffic tie-ups, irate bosses, unreasonable coworkers, a crashed computer, a surly teenager whose whereabouts are unknown, or a raging argument with a spouse. Although these occurrences don't threaten our survival in the literal sense, they are problematic enough to throw our sense of security and well-being into disarray.

Nonetheless, these modern-day stressors seem to activate our fight-or-flight response just as if we are facing a problem of life-threatening proportions. We're flooded with the same stress hormones that got our ancestors prepped for fight-or-flight. But if an irate boss is the problem, fighting or fleeing are usually not options. Far more likely, you have to coolly assess the situation and figure out your best move. A crashed computer may have you hopping mad—especially if you imagine vital files have been lost—but bashing it won't do much good. Whenever the fight-or-flight response is activated, we're likely to become aggressive and overreactive, ultrasensitive to negative signals, more likely to act impulsively, and less likely to think through the long-term consequences of our actions. In the words of Malcolm Gladwell, author of the recent bestseller *Blink*, we can become "mind-blind." And yet the fight-or-flight response sets in at the very time we most need to have a clear mind and a concern for the ultimate effects of our behavior. It's a conundrum.

As mentioned earlier, anger sometimes also includes a component of fear. When we are angry, we're responding to a *perceived threat* to our homeostasis. The operative term here is *perceived*. Imagine yourself in the shoes of a teenage boy who believes another guy is "hitting on" his girlfriend. If the teen is at all insecure about the relationship (as teens usually are), he may respond by rallying his defenses to challenge the rival. But deep down, he's fearful that this competitor may succeed in taking away someone he loves. Just as the hyperarousal of the fight-or-flight response can cloud our judgment, so can fear. Uncertainty leads us to misperceive, to interpret anything ambiguous as a threat. Even getting a dirty look from someone can create a sense of transgression, of violation: *What's on this person's mind? Can he do me harm?* Meanwhile, of course, the dirty look may well have been directed toward the guy next to you!

Studies have shown that even *talking* about something that made you angry can make you roughly half as angry as the anger-provoking threat itself. Anger recall is a well-documented phenomenon. In studies, when cardiac patients are asked to remember a recent incident that got them riled up, just describing the event in front of two white-coated health professionals caused their hearts to beat less smoothly and efficiently. Why does threat alone garner such a strong physiologic response? Because our potentially lifesaving fight-or-flight system is highly attuned to register subtle cues of possible danger. A disgusted sigh from a work supervisor, news that property taxes will be raised, or an unjust traffic summons could be enough to get those stress hormones flowing. And, primitive humans that we are, we are set to confront the Department of Motor Vehicles with as much ferocity as our ancestors fought a wolf in the wild.

How Our Environment Influences Anger Expression

We've seen how anger is both an infantile reaction and closely linked to a biologically programmed survival mechanism. But there is a third key factor that both shapes and determines how we express this anger. Our environment, the formative atmosphere that shapes our personality, may well be the strongest influence of all.

There is more than a grain of truth in the old expression "The apple doesn't fall far from the tree," especially when it comes to anger issues. From the time we are in the cradle, family members—especially parents—send us innumerable messages about what is expected of us; what we need to do to get our needs met; and how we are to think, act, and feel. They convey the message that certain traits and behaviors are to be encouraged and others are to be inhibited or denied. Parents are powerful role models for their children and offer a kind of blueprint for how strong emotions—particularly anger—are to be expressed.

As we have seen, anger is a universal emotion. But while all humans may experience anger, we learn to manage it differently—and to a striking degree, the lessons date back to what was demonstrated in our family. Some of us may openly yell and bellow, instinctively reverting to an adult version of the "terrible twos" ("I want what I want . . . and I want it *now!*"). Some may learn to hold negative emotions in check, seething under a carefully constructed facade of control ("No, really, I'm fine. There's nothing bothering me at all."). Others turn passive-aggressive—unable to express anger directly but nonetheless finding indirect ways to inflict pain. Imagine an unctuous president of the company at a board meeting stating, "Let's hear from Jim first and then we'll get to the interesting subjects," or a parent saying, "Was I supposed to drive you to that appointment? Oh my gosh, I *totally* forgot." Arriving late, spreading nasty rumors, or going back on an agreement are other time-honored ways of expressing indignation in an indirect way. Typically, the anger in such circumstances is outside the inflicting individual's awareness: "Really, I like Jim. I didn't mean anything at all by that comment. Why do you psychologists read into everything? Now, that's something to get me angry!"

By adulthood, we all have developed characteristic ways of dealing with anger. In other words, our method of expressing anger becomes part of our character. Often, our particular method of handling anger-provoking situations is modeled on the style of the same-sex parent. Young girls tend to adopt the traits of their mother or other primary female caregiver, while boys model themselves after their father or father figure and learn the "man's way" of expressing angry feelings, which is often spontaneous and direct. (This process will be explored more thoroughly in Chapter 3.)

Healthy Families Get Angry, Too

At this point, it may be worthwhile to remind you that there is nothing "wrong" with anger. It is a normal and healthy emotion. It is also an important signal that someone feels that something is wrong. In healthy families where children—and parents—are allowed to be their authentic selves, angry outbursts can actually be a mark of clear communication and a sign of trust. A child who can express anger appropriately is one who knows that he will still be loved even if he has a skirmish with a sibling or talks back to a parent on occasion. Likewise, parents who feel secure know they will not lose a child's love if they occasionally have to yell in order to set limits.

The child's job, by the way, is to test those limits, to discover what he can get away with, while the parent's job is to set those limits effectively. If a child is not "pushing the envelope," but instead relying on parental authority, he will become a follower—always looking to others for direction—rather than develop into an independent thinker.

Some people manage their anger appropriately, effectively, and without apparent difficulty. Those fortunate individuals most likely had the benefit of an upbringing where well-functioning role models showed that anger could be expressed in constructive ways, with a healthy respect for another person's boundaries and without the need to resort to verbal abuse, threats, manipulation, or physical violence. The rest of us may not have been so lucky, but that doesn't mean we can't revisit the issue in adulthood.

If you're reading this book, chances are you know what it's like to grapple with anger problems firsthand. Maybe, like the family in the beginning of this chapter, you sometimes find yourself overtaken by a helpless sense of rage—and then are shocked to realize you are treating your children in much the same way your mother treated you. Perhaps your moment of truth was similar to my own, when I realized I sounded like my father. You might have an anger style that leads you to use words like weapons and to say things that later make you cringe. Or you might realize that you use anger to get your desires met—bullying those who are less powerful and engaging in anger displays until family members give in to your demands. Without a doubt, you've also learned that the world is less tolerant of screaming adults than of crying infants.

So are most of us destined to be angry? Yes—and no. The truth is that while we humans all have a natural and even healthy capacity to experience anger, we don't come into the world stamped with a particular anger style: that is, a predetermined talent for raging, bellowing, or being passive-aggressive. How we manage anger is largely a learned behavior—and the lessons are absorbed, gradually and generally without our awareness, from our family of origin. Then when we become parents ourselves, we carry these influences of the past into our present-day relationships with our own children.

This cycle tends to continue—unless it is broken, because lessons learned about anger can be unlearned. With an adult's perspective, you can begin the process of re-addressing your own beliefs about this often puzzling emotion. And that sets the stage for creating a healthier, more loving legacy for your own children.

Now that we have reviewed a few of the origins of anger, let's take a closer look at anger itself: how it has been understood (and misunderstood) through the ages, how it gets passed down from generation to generation, and—most important—how to break that cycle of destructive rage once and for all.

Anger: Myths and Misunderstandings

How Your Beliefs About Anger May Influence How You Express Anger

Imagine yourself on a ship at sea, far from home port during a severe storm—before 1492, when the earth was still believed to be flat. As the wind takes hold of the sails and your ship careens toward the horizon, you may well be terrified that you will soon fall off the planet! Of course, we now know that there is no such possibility. Sailors today would be able to focus all their efforts on navigating through the storm, without the needless worry of meeting their doom at the edge of the earth. But the terror of a fifteenth-century sailor makes sense from his standpoint: it's a logical way of reacting, even though the belief is false.

Similarly, if you believe that your pent-up anger will cause you to "explode" at an inopportune moment—or that you will perhaps have a heart attack or stroke or develop high blood pressure by holding "so much" anger inside—you might well feel anxious if you don't "release" your anger. Our beliefs about reality help determine our actions; they play a central role in the choices we make and how we conduct our lives. But, as you will soon see, the myth that it is necessary to "vent" anger is as erroneous as the idea that the earth is flat.

Anger in Antiquity

Writers and philosophers have speculated about anger since early in human history. In Biblical times, "slowness to anger" was cited as a virtue in the Old Testament of the Bible (Proverbs 16:32): "He that is slow to anger is better than the mighty; and he that ruleth his spirit than he that taketh a city." Horace (65–8 B.C.), the Roman poet and satirist, said, "Anger is a momentary madness, so control your passion or it will control you."

Virtually all of the aphorisms and anecdotes that have been passed down from the early "sages of the ages" describe the difficulties inherent in managing anger and suggest that it can, indeed, get the best of us. A pervading myth of our times, however, says otherwise: "release your anger" or you will suffer negative consequences. How did this come to pass?

Anger and Aggression in Psychoanalytic Theory

It was not until the late nineteenth century that psychology became formally organized and scientific. Sigmund Freud, the father of modern psychoanalysis, offered some of the earliest comprehensive theories of the mind and mental illness. Many of Freud's concepts have been so deeply absorbed by our society that we simply take them for granted. Consider some of the terms that originated with psychoanalysis and are now a part of our collective vocabulary: the *unconscious*, the *ego*, the *id*, and the *superego*; *libido*, *repression*, *separation anxiety*, *sublimation*, *free association*, *transference*, *sibling rivalry*, and the *Oedipus complex*; *defense mechanisms* such as *denial*, *rationalization*, and *projection*; and psychological symptoms such as *obsessions* and *compulsions*. These terms are now part of our popular lexicon. And many of us continue to rely on them with as much belief in their certainty as our forebears had in their belief the earth was flat! Surprise: did you know you are a Freudian?

Curiously, Freud scarcely spoke about anger per se. In fact, there are only a handful of brief references to anger in the twenty-four-volume standard edition of his writings. Instead, he wrote extensively about the aggressive drive, which he thought to be far more basic to the human condition. According to Freud, we are all motivated by two basic biological drives: sex, or Eros, and aggression. He likened these drives to the forces of creation and destruction or attraction and repulsion in physics, and believed that every human act involves the interplay of these two competing drives. Our personalities—our egos—are always striving to find a workable balance between them.

So what is a drive? A drive is a "genetically determined excitation or tension that impels an individual to activity," an internal force that propels us to seek satisfaction. Note that a drive cannot be observed directly; it is inferred by behavior. Anger, in psychoanalytic theory, is an observable manifestation of the *presumed* aggressive drive. It's quite easy to observe behaviors that appear to be stimulated by our sex drive; indeed, the belief that we humans all have a sex drive is hardly questioned. However, the aggressive drive is another matter. In fact, many contemporary psychoanalysts and other psychological theorists no longer believe in the universal indigenous aggressive drive described by Freud and some of his followers.

Freud's theory of the aggressive drive is deeply pessimistic. He believed that we are all riddled with destructive and murderous impulses that originate in the id, the deepest part of our psyche. He described the id as "the dark, inaccessible part of our personality . . . a cauldron of seething excitations . . . [where] logical laws of thought do not apply." One way of obtaining a "window" on the id is through the play of young children, whose fantasies often emerge uncensored. When children play with war toys or squabble among themselves, they often have violent fantasies, threatening to "pull off" someone's head or "kill" their rivals. Another place we might infer the workings of the aggressive drive is through the violent video games so popular in our society. Children and adolescents (of any age) are widely drawn to the opportunity to mutilate and murder in fantasy. Freud believed such fantasies are universal—a manifestation of the aggressive drive.

Freud said that by adulthood, the vast majority of our aggressive impulses exist only in our imagination. Society could not function otherwise. He noted: "Restriction of the individual's aggressiveness is the first and perhaps the severest sacrifice which society requires." As we mature, the aggressive drive becomes sublimated: that is, channeled and refined as assertiveness, with the aim of achieving mastery over the environment, particularly in our careers. Aggression is also sublimated into healthy competition at school and in sports. Humor, which often contains an element of hostility, is another socially accepted sublimation.

Originally a neurologist, Freud was heavily influenced by biology. He believed the mind functioned in much the same way as the body and based his understanding of the aggressive drive on the model of the reflex. Humans have many reflexes: for instance, our pupils dilate and contract in response to light levels, and our knees jerk when stimulated by a doctor's hammer. Reflexes function involuntarily, automatically, and in an all-or-none fashion. Freud thought that the aggressive drive works similarly. He believed that it is as unwise to overly inhibit aggression as it is to repeatedly block the release of any other reflex.

Freud also believed that "psychic energy" is necessary to inhibit our aggressive impulses. (When very angry, have you ever had to contain your impulse to verbally or physically lash out at someone? It can take some effort.) He also believed the mind has only a limited supply of this energy; if it is expended in holding back aggression, less will be available for other activities. Too much inhibition is a bad thing. Indeed, Freud believed that some people have such a great inability to acknowledge and express anger that they direct it back at themselves: everything that goes wrong is their fault. Freud noted that depression is "anger turned inward."

Psychoanalysts have made use of another concept from physics to help explain the nature of the psyche in general and the aggressive drive in particular. The *hydraulic principle* was originally conceived by scientist-philosopher Blaise Pascal (1623–1662) back in the seventeenth century. Pascal's law states that *the pressure applied to a confined liquid is transmitted equally in all directions, regardless of the area to which the pressure is applied.* To envision this, picture a balloon filled with water. If you push in on the balloon with your finger, the shape of the entire balloon will change, not just the spot where your finger presses in. Too much force and the balloon might even rupture, spilling its contents all over.

Many psychoanalysts envision the workings of the mind in much the same way: each aspect of the psyche is intricately connected to every other, and pressure on one area will have an effect someplace else. Too much pressure from the aggressive drive may cause a "rupture" in the psyche, perhaps an emotional eruption—a child's temper tantrum or an adult's "anger attack"—or psychosomatic illness or some other undesirable consequence, just as if the balloon had burst. If you don't express your anger, the hydraulic model suggests it will manifest itself in some other way—perhaps in the ploy of coming home after a bad day at work and yelling at the children (an example of *displaced anger*). But, as you will see later, displacement is a faulty style of anger management; it's not caused by pent-up anger that needs to be released.

Think of the terms we automatically rely on to explain anger. We speak of *blowing up* or needing to *let off steam*; when anger mounts, we say that *pressure is building*. Sometimes we say we need to *vent*. Other times, we claim it's best to *let it all out*. But each term paints a picture of something physical, something that increases—some *thing* that seeks release. But anger is not a *thing*. It is a temporary emotion that lasts for a finite amount of time. There is no organ that stores this thing, no place in our bodies where anger accumulates. Isn't it amazing how the colloquial terms we use to describe anger so closely parallel Freud's ideas of the aggressive drive, the reflex model, and the hydraulic principle?

Psychoanalysis brought our inner lives out into the open; many subsequent styles of psychotherapy have extolled the virtues of "being in touch with yourself" and the importance of expressing emotions for the good of our relationships. Turn on any daytime TV talk show and you will see people acting on the belief that it is vital to "let their feelings out." To a large extent, we have benefited from this focus: relationships do require that we communicate effectively and know how other people feel. However, many people carry the idea too far, mistakenly venting in order to "relieve themselves" of what they believe is the pressure of pent-up anger.

Yes, it is often important to discuss what you are feeling. But the least effective time to do so is when you are very angry. It is far better to think things through before "blasting" someone, to be certain that you understand the circumstances not only from your perspective, but from the other person's as well.

So here, in a nutshell, is the confusion: many of us mistakenly equate anger with Freud's understanding of the operations of the aggressive drive. Since the days of Freud, the very existence of a universal aggressive drive has been challenged. In its place is the idea that anger is a reaction to circumstances. There is no *drive* inside of us that must be satisfied so we don't explode.

Differing Perspectives on Anger: Adler, Montagu, Klama

If Freud was the one who broke ground in establishing psychoanalysis and developing the first compre-

The Lexicon of Anger

Did you ever stop and wonder about the phrases we use to describe anger, and why so many of them refer to *building up, boiling over,* or the *need for release*? The aggressive drive, reflex model, and hydraulic principle are likely explanations of how this terminology has been passed down through the generations. Three-quarters of a century after Freud's heyday, we still use colloquialisms like these:

Pent-up anger
Built-up anger
Bottled-up anger
Getting steamed
Anger that spills over or leaks out
Anger that boils over
Letting it out
Letting someone have it
Pop off
Pop your cork
Exploding in anger
Blowing up
Blowing your top
Blowing your stack
Blowing off steam
Explosive rage
Volcanic rage

hensive theories of the mind and mental illness, a number of his contemporaries soon challenged some of his major ideas. One was Alfred Adler, a fellow psychotherapy pioneer in Vienna. Adler was the first psychological theorist to speak extensively about *anger*, as opposed to the aggressive drive, which was the focus of the day. He suggested that anger is a natural reaction that occurs whenever one of our primary drives is frustrated. Primary drives are biologically determined and include hunger and thirst and the needs for clothing, shelter, and a comfortable body temperature. For Adler, anger had a cause and effect; it was not something that happened automatically and involuntarily, like a knee-jerk reflex. Anger was not a biological drive.

Adler also offered new insights into the link between anger and personality. He noted that some individuals use anger to compensate for a feeling of inferiority through a seeming show of strength. Feelings of inferiority are universal, said Adler, a natural consequence of starting out life as a helpless, dependent infant. Adler believed that throughout childhood, the overriding sense of "inferiority, inadequacy, and insecurity" is commonplace and often amplified when caregivers demand more than a child is capable of doing, or if a child sees himself as physically weaker, less intelligent, or less attractive than his peers. Some people learn to cope by using anger as a kind of armor, Adler said. They feel weak, so they seek to project the opposite: a haughty, powerful, aggressive exterior. Acting aggressively can serve to intimidate an adversary in much the same way a four-legged creature can ward off a rival for its territory or mate by making itself seem frightening, for instance, by bellowing or charging.

Adler and many others have taken issue with Freud's theories of aggression. Ashley Montagu, a well-respected anthropologist whose career spanned the mid- to late twentieth century, offered some important new insights.

Freud was heavily influenced by Darwin's theory of natural selection, a major principle of which is *survival of the fittest*. In the animal kingdom, the biggest and most aggressive animals are most likely to win in the battle for nature's limited resources. Humans, too, sometimes need to display aggression to ensure survival. But Montagu saw things a bit differently. He noted that in the animal kingdom, aggression is most often expressed by a display of power rather than a literally destructive act. Most often, larger animals only need to demonstrate their superior strength with a gesture—think of a lion's roar or a bear standing on its hind legs. The gesture alone will ward off a rival. In fact, animals rarely kill one another except for food. And many species have a herding instinct, banding together to enhance their chances of survival—not by conquest, but through cooperation.

Montagu took a more benevolent view of human nature than did Freud. He rejected the idea that man is inherently "a killer" and argued instead that the expression of aggression comes primarily from *social learning*. While at birth we may all have the *potential* to turn violent, family and culture are the strongest determinants of whether or not we actually will. In fact, Montagu was an early proponent of the idea that the interpersonal environment plays the key role in shaping our personalities and our styles of anger expression.

In 1988, a diverse study group whose members came from the fields of anthropology, biology, history, political science, and psychology added more to the debate. John Klama (a pseudonym made up of the various authors' initials) also challenged the idea of a universal aggressive drive in their book, *Aggression: The Myth of the Beast Within*.

Like Montagu, Klama rejected the "man-as-killer" hypothesis. Moreover, the group questioned whether aggression has any validity at all as a scientific concept: the word has evolved into a handy, catch-all term to describe a wide range of assertive acts (people are said to walk, talk, even make love aggressively). Klama pointed out that aggression, certainly in popular usage, has become a "category of convenience," not necessarily a scientifically based "natural class of phenomena."

So if there is no aggressive drive, no "beast within" the human animal—where does our anger come from? Klama suggested that it is largely a developmental phenomenon. We are all shaped by a particular culture, one in which some behaviors are prized while others are punished; therefore "children learn what anger is, how they may be angry, and when their anger might be displayed; they learn how, when and why others may act aggressively; and they learn to cope with their own and other people's aggression." While it is true that children show differences in *temperament* from birth, Klama asserted that the differences are in *activity levels*, not aggressiveness. Klama stated that children are most likely to learn their "anger lessons" by example: the patterns of behavior displayed in a child's environment, and the way that child interacts with her most frequent caregivers, serve as models for learning *by imitation*. Authority figures—parents—are the ones a child is most likely to emulate.

Science: The Glue That Binds the Theories

The initial ideas about anger and the aggressive drive evolved largely from "armchair theorizing"—observations by psychologists and psychiatrists, often of their own admittedly troubled patients—rather than controlled, scientific investigations of behavior. It wasn't until the mid-1950s that scientific research on anger was actually begun. Many of the early scientific findings on anger—including family anger—emerged from the cardiac psychology literature.

A New Scientific Quest: Studying Anger's Generational Link

Some of the best research on the intergenerational transmission of anger comes from the Family Transitions Project, reported in 2003 by Rand Conger and Kee Jeong Kim at the University of California–Davis, and several of their colleagues at other universities, and published in the *Journal of Abnormal Child Psychology* in 2003. They studied angry, aggressive behavior across three generations in a cohort of 558 young people in rural Iowa. Adolescents were first interviewed in 1989 and again annually until 1999, when their average age was twenty-one to twenty-three. By 1999, 75 of the subjects had a child eighteen months of age or older. Of the study subjects, 451 came from two-parent families and 107 came from a single-parent family headed by a mother. Virtually all of the participants were Caucasian, lower- or middle-class, and young parents (21–23 years of age for the second generation, and their children averaged 2.4 years), limiting the generalizability of the results. Nonetheless, these are among the very best data in this area of study, utilizing multiple objective observations of parenting behaviors during structured interactions in participants' homes. The authors note that a social learning perspective predicts that, to a significant degree, people learn how to raise their children from their parents. Results "suggest a very robust and specific learning effect for parenting behavior" across three generations. The study finds good scientific support for what many have long suspected: "the apple doesn't fall far from the tree."

Do the ill effects of an angry family follow a person into adulthood? The evidence seems to suggest that they do. A study from the National Heart, Lung and Blood Institute, reported in 2000, looked at 2,525 adult children from 680 families. Dr. Gerdi Weiner and associates used the Cooke-Medley Hostility Scale, a questionnaire that has been utilized in many studies of hostility and coronary heart disease, and found a strong relationship between the quality of family relationships and *cynical hostility*—viewing the world as a cold, harsh place and the perceived need to "get others before they get you."

In 1996, Dr. Karen Matthews and her colleagues at the University of Pittsburgh explored the link between negative family interactions and later hostility in teenage boys. She observed fifty-one families and focused on how parents and sons attempted to resolve conflicts, testing the hypothesis that "family environments characterized as unsupportive, unaccepting, and conflictual lead to the development of hostile traits in adolescent boys." Dr. Matthews and her colleagues found that when fathers demonstrated many negative behaviors (or few positive behaviors), three years later their sons were more likely to display hostile attitudes, mistrust, and outward expression of anger.

Research with girls and their mothers supports a similar conclusion: a 1987 study reported in the *Jour-*

nal of Abnormal Psychology looked at girls with "conduct disorders" (in other words, violent behaviors). It not only showed that parents of these girls were more hostile than parents of nonviolent girls, but also that the relationship between parent and child hostility was strongest for the same-sex parent. The authors concluded, "Female children may be modeling the behavior of their parents, particularly that of their mothers."

From these studies and others, it does appear that anger and style of anger expression are transmitted in families. And the effects are evident when the children are studied as adults. Our understanding of anger in general, and family anger in particular, seemed to become clearer as the twentieth century drew to a close. Theorists from virtually every school of thought had come to rethink the psychoanalytic theory of a universal aggressive drive continually seeking expression. And yet, the misconception lingers—and can have lingering negative consequences.

Anger Myths: What You Believe *Can* Hurt You

Are you still wondering how beliefs about anger determine how we express this important emotion? If we don't "blow off steam," will we "blow up"?

Consider the case of Joan, a bright, attractive former actress; she is the divorced mother of three adult children and lives alone. When Joan suffered a stroke, requiring her to spend more than a week in the hospital, her daughter Tracy traveled from her home in another city to take care of her mother. From the start, though, Tracy made it clear that she could stay just two nights. She had to return home to give a major presentation at work.

When she heard Tracy's plans, Joan was indignant. Here she was, just out of the hospital and asking for her daughter's help—something she almost never did. And Tracy could stay only two nights because of work? How utterly self-centered!

In her state of self-righteous indignation, Joan decided to confront her daughter. "I can't believe you can be so selfish!" she yelled at Tracy, and then invoked an old issue: "This is the same kind of crap you pulled when you didn't pick me up for your brother's wedding." Tracy fired back, "Are you *still* harping about that? Well, I can't believe you still don't get what happened that day." The wedding, which had taken place many years earlier, continued to be a sore point between Joan and Tracy. The two had never cleared up the misunderstandings around this event.

On the day of the wedding, Joan had thought Tracy would transport her from her home to the ceremony, but her daughter never appeared. Fearing she would miss the wedding, Joan was forced to call a taxi at the last minute. When asked about the still-painful incident, Joan admitted that she wasn't sure whether her daughter had willfully left her in the lurch or whether there had been a communication error. But Joan continued to be angry about the episode and often made reference to it as evidence of her daughter's "completely selfish behavior."

The mother told her daughter to "pack your bag and get out!" Regardless, Tracy stayed one night. The mood was somber. Still indignant, Joan reported these events at her next group session, stating emphatically that she never wanted anything to do with Tracy again.

In relating the tale, Joan said that she felt she was "about to explode" and believed that if she didn't express her anger, "terrible things" might happen to her—maybe even another stroke. Joan said, "I couldn't shove that anger down in there." "Down where?" I pondered as group leader. There is no repository for anger in our bodies, no organ for storing it as we do with our waste products. Joan's belief—that she had to express her anger *no matter what*—directed her actions and resulted in bad feelings that will likely damage the mother-daughter relationship for a long time to come.

This anecdote is an example of how our beliefs about anger determine the ways we deal with it. But let's look at the situation from Joan's perspective. She had just been released from the hospital and felt very vulnerable. She needed someone to look after her. But she felt dismissed by Tracy (a variation on our theme of disrespect, as you will see later on), and thought her daughter's "excuse" for leaving was unduly selfish.

Tracy, on the other hand, felt quite differently. She had an important project and felt that her career might suffer if she stayed longer than two nights. Very often, as this example shows, anger is a matter of an individual's perspective.

So how might Joan have handled things more effectively? First, she might have appreciated her daughter's sacrifice rather than trivialize it. Perhaps Joan might have negotiated with Tracy, asking her if it was possible to stay just a little bit longer. Most critically, Joan might have seen that her wish for companionship could be fulfilled in a variety of ways. She needed someone to look after her, but there were choices available other than her daughter. In fact, after Tracy left, Joan called in a visiting nurse for a few days, ultimately fulfilling her requirement for support in this way.

Notice, too, how Tracy reacted similarly to her mother: they both were stuck on seeing the situation from their own perspective. This situation ended badly: mother and daughter did not speak with one another for a long time, and there was a "chill" in their conversation when they finally did manage to resume talking.

In tackling anger management, it is important to realize that we have little choice about filling our *needs*, but considerable flexibility when it comes to managing our *wants*. As you will see repeatedly throughout this book, *need fulfillment* is at the heart of anger management—and the capacity to fill our needs is a hallmark of maturity.

Imagine being a parent like Joan, who believes that bad things will happen to her if she doesn't express her anger. Perhaps she will have another stroke or a heart attack because of all the "built-up tension." Imagine, further, being the child of such a parent: you too will believe that you have to express your anger in order to avoid "exploding" or developing an illness. Now imagine being a fly on the wall in the home of these individuals when there is a disagreement: everyone believes she *has to* express her anger. There will nearly always be a negative atmosphere, with lots of yelling and screaming and many unresolved differences. It's easy to see that this belief will, in many instances, be transferred from one generation to the next, parents teaching children the "critical importance" of venting. Unfortunately, this is the state of affairs in many households today.

Even My Wife and Daughter Needed Convincing of How Anger Really Works

The myth of the importance of expressing anger is so widespread I even encounter it in my own family. One night at home, I sat down with my wife and twelve-year-old daughter to relax together and share the events of the day. I talked about this book and its main hypothesis: that it's *not* necessary to express anger.

Both my wife and daughter looked at me with shock and disbelief. "Doesn't anger build up?" said my wife, Amanda. Sara, my daughter, queried, "Isn't it really important to let it out?" They both got annoyed at me for thinking otherwise. How could I possibly question something so obvious?

Sara then described a classmate who frequently bothered her. "Practically no one in the class likes her," my daughter confided. "She's mean and a pest." Each time the classmate did something that troubled her, Sara felt more and more annoyed. The question, however, is whether the anger was building up inside of Sara (as my daughter and wife believed) or whether the anger was increasing as a result of repeated exposures to this classmate's irritating behaviors.

Learning theory long ago demonstrated that the intensity of our reactions to negative stimuli is directly linked to how frequently we encounter them. Sometimes we even provide our own "repeated exposure" to anger-provoking experiences by replaying them in our minds. Whenever we mentally relive the experience of another person's cutting remark or annoying behavior, it serves as another exposure. And, as previously noted, describing situations that made you angry has such dramatic, demonstrable results that it has become an experimental technique for studying the effects of anger on the heart.

The fact is, a stimulus-response formulation is more accurate than the idea that anger accumulates: we become angrier with *repeated exposures* to anger-provoking events. Anger does not build up inside of us, although it may feel that way when you once again encounter a person or situation that has triggered your anger in the past. This fact is critically important because, for many of us, how we understand anger determines how we ultimately manage it.

Watchful Eyes: Anger in the Family Is Seen, Heard, and Felt

How well I remember the experience, growing up, of watching my dad lose his temper. We weren't always sure what would set him off—it could be anything from a chore left undone to a haircut that was not to his liking. Even though his outbursts could be unpredictable, they seemed to occur with a frightening regularity.

When I was in eighth grade, my dad caught me smoking cigarettes. To "teach me a lesson," he started to spank me, and with each indignant "I'll teach you to smoke!" he became more and more enraged. At first, my mother stood quietly on the sidelines. But as the whacks started to escalate, she began to scream. My sister ran off to hide in a closet. I may have been the object of my father's anger at that particular moment, but his fury resonated throughout the entire household. While hitting me, my father seemed to go into a daze, almost intoxicated by the elixir of my helplessness and his rage. The final irony: he was a smoker!

Knowing how it felt to be brutalized by my father, I vowed I would never treat my own children this way. So how did it happen that I, as a young adult, sometimes found myself feeling and acting as angrily as he did? Where did this anger come from? Why would I, of all people, exhibit some of the very same traits I disliked so much in my father? The short answer: I learned it at home.

Anger and the Identification/Imitation Process

By now, most contemporary behavior experts agree that how we come to express anger is, in large part, a learned process. But why, precisely, does a child learn to express anger in much the same manner as a parent—particularly if he or she grew up victimized by that parent's wrath? Why would a youngster take on those very same traits for him- or herself?

In young children, lessons learned about anger (and a host of other personality traits) are largely acquired through the twin processes of identification and imitation. Simply put, *identification* is a means by which children become like their same-sex parent—

and they do that, in large part, by the *imitation* of that parent's behavior. For instance, a little girl sees her mother admiring her jewelry in the mirror, shopping for clothes, reading, studiously working at the computer, or organizing volunteer food drives—engaging in virtually any activity—and she begins to act much the same way, to follow similar patterns. Or a little boy sees his father watching football, tinkering with tools, or spending hours bent over spreadsheets, and he too begins to emulate this kind of behavior.

By now, the concepts of identification and imitation have become well-established tenets of social learning theory. The germ of the idea originated, yet again, with Sigmund Freud. Freud believed most children identify with their same-sex parent and imitate many of their patterns of behavior. Freud viewed this task—in which a child incorporates the same-sex parent's beliefs, behaviors, and attitudes into his own emerging personality—as part of the way humans forge gender identity. Scholars from different fields of expertise have come to view identification and imitation as key developmental processes. By the middle of the twentieth century, social psychologists, such as Alfred Bandura and the working group Klama (see Chapter 2), regarded these processes from the perspective of social learning theory: simply put, we become what we observe.

Not only do children observe different types of anger in childhood, but they also learn ways to deal with their own anger in these crucial, formative years—and typically, these methods of anger management become adaptive strategies that follow us through adulthood. Some children may react to angry parents by becoming aggressive and hostile themselves, expressing those traits at home and in the world at large. Others might adopt the opposite approach: they become overly timid and eager to please. Clearly, the key influences on a child's developing personality seem to be patterns of behavior and interactions with significant people that are repeated again and again. But other factors also come into play: temperament, birth order, a traumatic experience, an early separation, a supportive mentor, experiences of success or failure—all these variables help shape who we are. Just as no two children share exactly the same upbringing, no two people respond to their upbringing (including an *angry* upbringing) in precisely the same way.

Growing Up with Angry Parents: What Young Children Observe

Imagine being three, four, or five years old, growing up in an angry household. A young child has no frame of reference beyond his immediate environment. He is not yet able to look at parents' angry outbursts and objectively decide *My father is overreacting* or *My mother is really mad at something else and she is taking it out on me.* Instead, the youngster quietly absorbs all the messages he sees around him about how adults

Are There More Angry Men than Women?

Are men angrier than women? Perhaps. In my practice, I often treat cardiology patients referred because a physician believes that anger problems could heighten their risk of a heart attack. Gender identification may be one reason why I see more men than women who fit this profile.

Traditionally, men have been taught to express their anger in direct, forceful ways, all part of the "dominant male" role so prized in our culture. Anger is equated with strength. Get angry, be assertive, and you will get what you want: so the logic goes. Even if we consciously choose to ignore this directive, we still tend to model our own anger style after that of the same-sex parent or parental figure. For a young boy growing up, Dad sets the example; gender identification is typically encouraged by fathers and reinforced by mothers to ensure the son's masculinity. By puberty, this patterning has become internalized; if a boy sees that anger works for Dad, he's apt to believe it will work for him too. The angry-male pattern is likely to be further reinforced at school, where a boy may be considered a "wimp" if he lets himself get bullied by others, but a "hero" if he initiates a show of strength. Over a lifetime, gender-based socialization tends to forge a recognizable pattern of typical male anger in our culture—along with some of the corresponding cardiovascular risks.

Psychologists are actively studying extremes of this type of behavior: "super-masculine" men. Such individuals have a great desire to be dominant, focus on competition and success, have a fear of intimacy, restrict their positive behavior with other men, and—perhaps not surprisingly—have high levels of hostility. One recent study reported that the higher men scored on a scale that assesses this pattern, the higher their depressive symptoms and the lower their measures of marital adjustment. Not surprisingly, higher scores were also associated with wives' lower marital satisfaction as well.

behave. Parents are, quite literally, their children's first teachers, and their lessons make a huge impact.

Perhaps a young boy witnesses his father engaging in angry outbursts any time he doesn't get his way; Dad bullies everyone in the household and leaves the rest of the family intimidated and fearful. A young boy with such a role model will observe that intimidating people with anger is a good way to get your demands met (it certainly works for Dad). This is one common example of how children identify with the same-sex parent—and become like that parent by imitating the parent's actions and incorporating the parent's beliefs. If the child is rewarded for acting like his father—if Mom and his siblings cave in to his demands—his behavior is reinforced and he is well on his way to becoming like Dad. Or maybe a little girl grows up in a household with a mother who doesn't cope well with frustration. When life becomes stressful, Mom lashes out—with sarcastic comments, abusive accusations, or even the occasional painful slap. The entire family responds by walking on eggshells, trying to keep Mom placated and avoiding anything likely to push her buttons. What does a daughter learn? *My mom's anger gives her a lot of power; everybody does what she wants. When I get big, if I act like she does I'll be just as powerful.*

It is important to realize, though, that children don't make a calculated decision to follow in an angry parent's footsteps. When experts speak of this as learned behavior, they aren't referring to a classroom-type process in which youngsters scrutinize facts and absorb new knowledge. Instead, the process just happens: identification and imitation occur on a subconscious level.

Anger in Disguise

Of course, anger isn't always expressed in the form of temper tantrums or fierce tirades. Often, parents mask their anger behind a host of other behaviors, and children are indelibly influenced by these as well. Passive-aggressive tactics, unusually judgmental stances, and emotional withdrawal are prime examples of anger in disguise.

The Passive-Aggressive Parent. Some parents don't engage in angry outbursts; in whatever they do, they try to be "nice." But somehow, they manage to express their hostility in indirect ways; for instance, by failing to follow through on agreements, by "forgetting" promises made to a child, or by making cutting remarks behind that child's back. Such individuals often will not acknowledge that they are angry. Instead, they deal with things passive-aggressively. Their *actions* are hostile, but usually camouflaged with an attitude of being "nice" or "helpful."

Passive-aggressive parents are likely to send their children a variety of confusing mixed messages. Sometimes their words are contradictory: "You look beautiful in that dress! Now, if you can just remember to hold your stomach in . . ." The child may well be left wondering, *Do I look great, or do I look fat? And if my mother is trying to make me feel good, why do I feel awful?* In other instances, a parent's words seem to be at odds with their actions. Suppose a father tells his child, "It's important that you work hard and get an A on that test," but then refuses to turn down the TV or puts on loud music while the child needs quiet to study. The youngster might think, *If my dad wants me to succeed, why won't he cooperate with me?* Often, a child subjected to this kind of passive-aggressive parenting begins to think, *I can't win no matter what I do.* Perhaps he gives up trying.

Sometimes, as children struggle to make sense of conflicting messages, they may begin to adopt some passive-aggressive techniques of their own. For instance, a youngster might become an underachiever at school in response to her parents' mixed messages about academic accomplishment. Without overtly telling parents *I'll get even with you!*, she has found a way to express her anger by becoming polite but non-compliant (a passive-aggressive behavior) about a matter her parents regard as important.

The Judgmental Parent. Some of the angriest people I know are also the most judgmental. However, they typically do not even know they are angry. Instead of acknowledging their anger, they take a stance of extreme righteousness in the moral, political, or religious arena, to name a few—ready to do battle with anyone who challenges their beliefs. Quick to label others' actions (including their children's) as *bad*, *immoral*, or *ridiculous*, they are rarely able to see both sides of an issue and are unwilling to compromise or to admit that they do not necessarily have all the answers.

I recall once giving a lecture in a Midwestern city and speaking to the audience about the risk factors for heart disease, including diet, stress, and anger. In this

When Children Keep Secrets

When parents are chronically angry, children often react by becoming secretive. The child learns that hiding a bad test grade or sneaking a "forbidden" video is an effective way to ward off anticipated reactions from parents who might be overtly hostile, judgmental, or passive-aggressive. Keeping secrets is a way for the child to keep his behavior private and his vulnerabilities shielded. But when secret-keeping becomes a way of life, the entire family gets caught in a pattern of deceit, in which issues are never addressed honestly and directly.

When a parent is angry at a child's behavior, *recognizing and acknowledging that fact* is far better than subjecting the child to a barrage of harsh criticism. That allows parent and child to tackle the real issue of whether the youngster's behavior is self-defeating and how it might be corrected. For instance, if a child stays up too late at night or spends too much time with video games, it is worthwhile to ask why this is happening rather than merely telling the child his actions are "bad." Parents might be surprised at what they discover. Perhaps the child is having difficulty with a particular subject (accounting for the late nights). Or maybe he had an upsetting day at school. When given a choice, children will usually assume responsibility for their behavior—particularly when they come to realize that keeping secrets instead of addressing problems will not help get them what they want. Telling a child what to do is generally not as helpful as pointing out how he can act more effectively.

laid-back community, far from my own bristly hometown of Manhattan, the attendees looked puzzled. *Angry? Us?* After the talk, a farmer came up to me, stuck his index finger in my chest, and (apparently objecting to my dietary advice about limiting red meat consumption) said, "Listen, Mister Smarty-Pants New Yorker, do you really think we can get rid of the cattle ranches and just grow soybeans out here?" He wouldn't consider the idea that I had no agenda regarding anyone's cattle-rearing livelihood; I was merely talking about health effects and cardiovascular risks. To him, I represented the enemy. Yet amazingly, despite his tirade, he had no idea that he was angry.

Of course, many well-intentioned people hold passionate beliefs. What sets the angry, judgmental person apart is his unwillingness to be questioned or challenged, usually coupled with an attitude that anyone who disagrees with him is wrong.

So how does it feel to be a child who has this kind of parent as a role model? Right from the start, the youngster likely absorbs the idea that it's dangerous to disagree: he is not allowed to question, ponder, or challenge the status quo. He may identify with a parent's rigid way of thinking and strive to live up to whatever tenets Mom or Dad represent: Our religion is the right one. If you are not a Democrat, you're warmongering and narrow-minded. If you are not a Republican, you're wimpy and disloyal to the flag. Or, as the offspring of my Midwestern farmer might have surmised, those smarty-pants New Yorkers have no right to tell us how to live! Perhaps the child perceives a certain security that comes with living within the boundaries of an unwavering, codified belief system: it not only provides ready answers to all of life's complexities, but allows him to win the approval of his all-knowing parents.

But there *is* a flip side: how does it feel when the child is on the receiving end of parents' harsh appraisals? What happens when Dad rails against his son for being a "sissy" because he does not like football? Or when a mother labels her six-year-old "disgusting" because she asks a few honest questions about where babies come from? A child can be judged for being too messy, too loud, too disrespectful, too fat, not studious enough . . . the list goes on and on. What do all these judgments have in common? They assail the child's character, rather than constructively addressing his actions. Often, they come from a parent whose own anger is unacknowledged—masked as judgmental condemnation.

Certainly, the ability to make sound judgments is an admirable quality. But it is the tendency to rely on judgments, rather than acknowledging emotions, that can be a major source of family strife. Judgments tend to limit discussion. If a parent calls a child *stupid* or says his behavior is *bad* or *immoral*, it does not invite dialogue about what is motivating the behavior or how it might be improved. Things are left at a stalemate.

The Withdrawing Parent. The withdrawal of approval is another powerful weapon parents can use against children—and for a helpless, dependent youngster, the prospect can be terrifying. Being uninterested in a child's activities, needs, or accomplishments or using words like "I really don't care what you do" can be another form of anger in disguise. And it cuts right to the core of a child's sense of self-worth. Some parents flatly refuse to communicate, perhaps by leaving the room or smugly saying "The subject is closed!" when the child has something vital to say. Others employ the silent treatment, freezing the child out. Similar to passive-aggressive and judgmental behaviors, *withholding* tactics serve to hurt or manipulate the child, but in a way that is less direct than an outright angry tirade. Yet the impact can be even more devastating than a physical slap.

In response, some children develop the stance that they must get their parents' approval, no matter how they do it. Even in adulthood, and in a variety of life circumstances, the need for approval may continue to be an overriding motivation. That child is likely to develop a host of defenses to ward off rejection: he might become overly compliant because experiencing disapproval is just too painful. He may become withdrawn himself, deciding it's not safe to look to anyone for emotional support. Or he might become needy and dependent, always striving to find a way to keep some form of emotional sustenance intact—regardless of any negative consequences.

The Angry Parent *Never* Thinks He or She Is at Fault

Children who grow up where anger is rampant and encouragement is in short supply may react in a variety of ways, but they tend to share one distinct disadvantage as they grow to adulthood. They often have difficulty giving themselves the supportive words they need, because they did not get the chance to *imitate* and *internalize* a nurturing voice. What they internalized, instead, is a caustic voice that always criticizes and lashes out.

Another problem that compounds the dilemma of a child growing up in such a household is this: angry people are rarely willing to admit *they* might be the source of a problem. It's the rest of the world that needs to change! Instead of taking responsibility for what they bring to a situation, angry people typically lash out in every other direction: resenting the boss who is too demanding, the spouse who can't get organized, or the child who is always an easy and ready target.

Typically in angry families, the dominant parent engages in a pattern of finger-pointing and fault-finding, subjecting the child to an endless barrage of criticism: *What's wrong with you? Why can't you do anything right? If it weren't for you, we wouldn't have this problem!* Since this parent is the undisputed tyrant of the family, he or she is rarely criticized; frankly, he or she is just too intimidating. The victims of this rage—spouse and children—are usually too browbeaten to stand up for themselves. They often remain paralyzed by the fear that they will be victimized yet again.

I recall one patient, Frederick, who fit this profile of "winning through intimidation." He was an aggressive, financially successful first-generation storeowner from Eastern Europe who continually railed against his wife and children for not being more respectful. Though Frederick had married an American wife, his model for the ideal family was based on old-world values. He extolled the virtues of nearby Indian and Chinese shopkeepers; in these families, the father's word was law and his authority went unquestioned. Wives would obediently shop, cook, and clean; sons were expected to work long hours in their fathers' stores for no pay.

But Frederick's two sons, George and Richard, were protected from his "dirty" business (secondhand clothing) by his upstart American wife, Pauline; they rarely set foot in the store. Frederick disdainfully referred to his sons as "the girls" and berated them for showing him so little respect (of course, his own treatment of them was anything but respectful). Home was never a happy place. George and Richard tried to avoid their father, often hiding in their rooms until he left for work and scurrying back when he came home. Richard, the younger sibling, became phobic—so fearful that he refused to attend school.

Frederick blamed all these troubles on his wife: "If only Pauline were more respectful, the kids would be too!" he complained. "Then I wouldn't be so angry." Words like *if only* are a good tip-off that you may be unaware of your contribution to an angry situation; there will always be circumstances on which you can "pin" your anger or a circumstance that wouldn't be so upsetting *if only* something were different. Curiously, Frederick chose a liberal American wife when he could have easily attracted one who was far more traditional. This pattern is not unusual: angry people sometimes have a way of unwittingly setting up the very circumstances they claim are the root of their problems. So Frederick and his family remained trapped in a never-ending cycle of blame and fault-finding; problems never got resolved and the quality of family time never improved. Over time, Pauline and the boys developed ways of dealing with Frederick's rage, most often avoiding him. This was one unhappy family with emotional scars for all—including a father who felt isolated and unloved, in large part because of his own anger.

The Punishment Paradox

Virtually all parents (even angry ones) want to see their children grow up to be happy, secure, high-functioning adults. Most have their children's best interests at heart. At the same time, parents quickly come to realize that children do need guidance and direction—or *discipline*—so they will develop effective, healthy ways to live. The word *discipline* is derived

The Fixers

If a family includes a dominant, angry male, wives and daughters sometimes inadvertently become the "fixers." They may or may not feel responsible for the angry behavior, but their nurturing tendencies fuel their desire to make everything better. These are the women who are always trying to please, who can never say no, who blame themselves whenever anything goes wrong. Trying to be all things to all people, they themselves sometimes end up angry and depressed.

from *disciple*, which means *a follower* or *a learner*. In popular use, though, discipline is often equated with harsh punishment. Axioms such as "spare the rod and spoil the child" drive home the idea that stern punishment is a justified, necessary aspect of parenting.

Angry adults are especially quick to adopt a misguided notion of discipline in order to justify their methods for doling out harsh punishment. But they also tend to punish when they are most angry—a time when judgment is notoriously clouded—not necessarily when the child's behavior is most in need of correction. Punishments can be driven more by the parent's rage than from a well-thought-out strategy designed to guide and instruct the child.

One night in a restaurant, I couldn't help noticing a five-year-old girl and her parents seated at the next table. The child seemed noisy and demanding (not unusual for a five-year-old, I told myself) but she was also quite rude to the waiter: "I wanted *red* jello, not green. You're stupid!" Instead of correcting her daughter's manners, the mother seemed oblivious and even slightly amused by the antics. Gradually, though, that amusement faded as the meal progressed and Mom's patience waned. When the child (coloring her placemat by this time) whined because she had broken a crayon, the mother finally lost it: "Shut up! Just *shut up!*" she screamed as she proceeded to spank the little girl.

Such scenes are disturbingly typical in angry families—although most often the outbursts take place behind closed doors. In such circumstances, children are usually powerless and filled with silent rage. Far from learning whatever "lesson" the parent hoped to impart, the child may be totally confused: *What did I do wrong? Why did my mother laugh when I talked back to a waiter, but scream when I was upset because I broke a crayon?* From the child's viewpoint, there is no logical cause-and-effect sequence between what she does and how her parent reacts.

That sense of frustration is sometimes compounded by an overwhelming fury at being the victim of such treatment: *If I were as big as you I'd hit you right back! I'll get even with you someday. . . .* At present, though, the child has few options. She can't very well overpower an abusive parent or pack up and leave. But what she *can* do, sadly, is internalize the negative message, perhaps starting to believe that she is a bad person. She may begin to direct some of the anger her parents imparted back at herself. Indeed, Freud long ago noted that depression is "anger turned inward." At the same time, the child has a firsthand demonstration (again, from her parents) of how to take that anger out on others. And so the cycle continues.

How We Can Lose Touch with Our Own Anger

One common consequence of growing up in an angry family—or a family that was so strict that you were

When Does Anger Become Abuse?

Yelling, sarcasm, verbal slurs, physical slaps—what all abusive gestures have in common is the desire to inflict pain. If a parent tells a child, "I was furious that you got home two hours late when you knew your curfew was midnight!" the parent is addressing the child's behavior, not the child's character. The youngster is getting feedback on how his actions were inappropriate and what effect they had. But the comment "You're a stupid, irresponsible idiot!" offers no dialogue. Instead, the goal is to *make the child feel bad about himself*—either because the parent is experiencing unbridled rage in the moment or because he believes that guilt and shame will motivate the child to change his ways. Yet these kinds of remarks, over time, constitute the kind of abuse that causes deep and lasting damage to self-image.

not permitted to criticize or challenge your parents— is that you may not be fully aware of just how angry you really are. In an environment that is hostile or hurtful, children may learn to rid themselves of unpleasant thoughts by avoiding them—literally banishing them from conscious awareness.

Freud used the term *repression* to signify this sort of motivated forgetting, invoking the idea that "psychic energy" is required to keep the thoughts unconscious. The process can become debilitating, Freud thought. An overly repressed individual may develop psychological symptoms, such as excessive fears or compulsions, indicating that this buried energy is seeking another outlet.

Repression is a very common defense mechanism, but one that makes you "lose touch" with what you really feel. When something is repressed it is banished from consciousness; repressed anger is beyond awareness. By contrast, a suppressed thought is something you are conscious of but choose to keep to yourself. Suppressed anger is a choice; you know you are angry but choose not to express it.

Regardless of the accuracy of Freud's theory of repression, experts from different behavioral specialties are well acquainted with the "forgetting" that often occurs with traumatic events; it is a major symptom of posttraumatic stress disorder. Vietnam veterans often cannot recall many distressing experiences of wartime, and only reclaim those memories years later, if at all—hopefully in the nurturing comfort of psychotherapy. Physicians frequently see patients who have endured great physical pain, but as little as a few days afterward are unable to remember how badly they felt. Accident victims are also subject to this process. Far from being pathological, this type of "forgetting" is a very common phenomenon: if the emotional pain of an event is too great, the memory of it can often become inaccessible.

Early memories are very formative and some of the most powerful we ever experience. Yet if those recollections include insults and injuries, cowering in fear when we crossed paths with an enraged mother or father, our brains may find a way to forget it ever happened. We literally do not know how much pain we might have felt or how angry we were.

The Legacy Continues: How an Angry Childhood Can Affect Lifelong Health

The effects of growing up with angry parents aren't easily shaken off. Quite the contrary: there is mounting evidence that spending formative years in a hostile environment can have lifelong ill effects on your physical health.

My personal interest in anger in the family didn't originate just from my father's emotional outbursts, but also from the distressing fact that he had his first heart attack at age forty-six. I did not want to end up the same way. Indeed, anger has long been associated with coronary heart disease, and some of the findings on family anger have come out of those studies.

In the late 1950s, two San Francisco cardiologists, Drs. Meyer Friedman and Ray Rosenman, first identified an "action-emotion complex" they termed the *type A behavior pattern*. The term *type A* is now a household word for hard-driven, high-strung activity.

The concept originated from a number of studies that provided the first scientific links between psychological stress and heart attacks. The two major symptoms of type A behavior are easily aroused anger (termed *free-floating hostility*) and time pressure (doing too much in too little time).

Friedman and Rosenman further noted that some individuals manifest certain personality traits—particularly easily aroused anger—that predispose them to create "stress" out of nearly any situation, even harmless ones. For such individuals, even mundane events such as traffic jams or music preferences can be a major stress-inducer.

Carrying this idea further, one of the major theories in cardiac psychology, the *cardiovascular reactivity hypothesis*, suggests that some people frequently perceive many harmless situations as personally threatening and respond with chronic heightened sympathetic nervous system activity.

You will recall the "fight-or-flight" response first cited in Chapter 1 (and initially described more than sixty years ago by an eminent Harvard experimental physiologist, Walter B. Cannon). To quickly recap: whenever we perceive danger, a host of physiologic responses kick into gear, getting our bodies ready to confront danger. Our heart and respiration rates rise, along with our blood pressure. The "stress hormones," adrenaline and cortisol, are secreted to power our large muscles and heighten the acuity of vision and hearing. Our platelets get "sticky," meaning that blood can clot more easily so we won't bleed to death in the event of injury. We stop digesting food, too. This is a holdover from the days when humans fled from wild animals; the physiologic wisdom is *Who needs to digest lunch when you're about to* become *lunch?*

Fight-or-flight is designed to put our body into a state of high alert, something that enhances our chance for survival in a life-threatening situation. That is very beneficial in the short term. However, over-activation of the fight-or-flight response—in other words, over the long term—may injure blood vessels and promote the accumulation of artery-clogging plaque. If you are nearly always in a state of hyper-arousal, such stress may have effects on the body that nature never intended—particularly if those stress hormones are circulating freely while you seethe in traffic or fume over a computer, rather than metabo-lizing during fight-or-flight. Scientists are still study-ing the ways in which chronic excess cardiovascular reactivity may damage coronary arteries.

We do know from scientific research that intense anger can trigger the plaque rupture that is responsi-ble for most heart attacks. Approximately 1.3 percent of heart attacks—and likely, a similar percentage of sudden deaths—are triggered by intense anger. While that may seem like a small percentage, it translates to roughly *thirteen thousand* heart attacks per year in the United States—hardly insignificant if you or a loved one happen to be one of those stricken.

There is also mounting evidence that chronic stress does more than damage the heart. If physiologic changes associated with the fight-or-flight response become part of the grind of daily living (in other words, if the "stress switch" is stuck in the half-on position), it might eventually contribute to a suppressed immune system and even susceptibility to the common cold. Scientists still have many unanswered questions about the complexities of the mind-body connection, and they continue to explore mechanisms by which psychological stress may contribute to disease.

Eyes on the Prize: Effective Anger Management

In Part 1 of this book, you most likely have discovered the source of your anger, why you express it the way you do, and how that particular mode of expression might be passed on to your own children. Understanding how particular patterns of behavior develop can be helpful in bringing about constructive change.

In Part 2, you will find out how to make that change happen. Since anger expression is, at least in part, a learned process, the good news is that destructive patterns of anger expression can be replaced by healthier, more effective forms of anger management. By understanding the mechanisms of what triggers anger, and adopting a way of responding that respects both you and others, you will be well on the way to eradicating some of the harmful behavior patterns of your past. In a very real sense, you will be breaking the cycle that keeps families locked into the same dysfunctional behavior generation after generation—and creating a newer, healthier family legacy.

Part **II**

Breaking the Cycle

Dr. Allan's Anger Management Formula

Consider the following fable from Carol Tavris's groundbreaking 1982 book—one of the first to explore the topic of anger—entitled *Anger: The Misunderstood Emotion*:

On the train to Brindavan a swami sits beside a common man who asks him if indeed he has attained self-mastery, as the name *swami* implies.

"I have," says the swami.

"And have you mastered anger?"

"I have."

"You mean you can control your anger?"

"I can."

"And you do not feel anger?"

"I do not."

"Is this the truth, Swami?"

"It is."

After a silence the man asks again, "Do you really feel that you have mastered your anger?"

"I have, as I told you," the swami answers.

"Then do you mean to say, you never feel anger, even—"

"You are going on and on—what do you want?" the swami shouts. "Are you a fool? When I have told you—"

"Oh, Swami, this is anger. You have not mas—"

"Ah, but I have," the swami interrupts. "Have you not heard about the abused snake? Let me tell you a story.

"On a path that went by a village in Bengal, there lived a cobra who used to bite people on their way to worship at the temple there. As the incidents increased, everyone became fearful, and many refused to go to the temple. The swami who was master at this temple was aware of the problem and took it upon himself to put an end to it. Taking himself to where the snake dwelt, he used a mantra to call the snake to him and bring it into submission. The swami then said to the snake that it was wrong to bite the people who walked along the path to worship and made him promise sincerely that he would never do it again.

"Soon it happened that the snake was seen by a passerby upon the path, and it made no move to bite him. Then it became known that the snake had some-how been made passive and people grew unafraid. It was not long before the village boys were dragging the poor snake along behind them as they ran laughing here and there.

"When the temple swami passed that way again, he called the snake to see if he had kept his promise. The snake humbly and miserably approached the swami, who exclaimed, 'You are bleeding! Tell me how this has come to be.' The snake was near tears and blurted out that he had been abused ever since he was caused to make his promise to the swami.

"'I told you not to bite,' said the swami, 'but I did not tell you not to hiss.'"

An Effective Starting Point for Anger Management

While this appears to be a whimsical story, the swami tale delivers a strong central message: biting may be off-limits, but there is nothing wrong with an appropriate hiss. In fact, knowing the difference between a "hiss" and a "bite" might be the best starting point in managing anger effectively.

Good anger management isn't a matter of veering from one extreme (yelling and screaming) to the other (lying down and docilely accepting abuse, like the hapless snake). Instead, it is the challenge of learning when, how, and under what circumstances to effectively "hiss"—that is, to stand firm and issue a warning that certain behavior is unacceptable. A hiss might include a clear statement of what the consequences will be if that behavior continues, such as "I won't talk to you until you're ready to speak more calmly" or "You can't go to the mall until the lawn is mowed." Notice that this tactic is very different from lashing out with an aggressive "bite." A "hiss" is a *warning sign*; it says, "Watch out, pay attention!" whereas a "bite" is *any action intended to inflict pain.*

When I work with patients on their anger management issues, we define the difference between a bite and a hiss. From there, I offer a set of five clearly defined rules, which I call "Dr. Allan's Anger Management Formula." These guidelines form a step-by-step plan designed to help break the cycle of hurtful, inappropriate, and ineffective displays of fury so that you can gradually adopt anger management tools that work.

More than two thousand years ago, the philosopher Aristotle observed, "Anyone can become angry— that is easy. But to be angry with the right person, to the right degree, at the right time, for the right purpose, and in the right way—that is *not* easy." How can you begin to navigate this challenge more effectively? Start with these five rules. They are guideposts designed to give you sure footing every step of the way.

Rule Number One

Don't react in anger; respond instead.

This rule follows the belief that it's nearly always better to *manage* anger than to express it directly. A planned response will almost always be far more effective than a reactive outcry. The popular wisdom of not making important decisions "when you are emotional" is often a reference to anger.

If you stop and consider how it feels to be furious in the moment, it's not hard to understand where the term *in the heat of anger* comes from. Anger makes us fiery and intense—unable to think with a clear or cool head. As the French philosopher-essayist Montaigne said back in the sixteenth century, "There is no passion that so shakes the clarity of our judgment as anger. Things truly seem different to us once we have quieted and cooled down."

When we react in anger, we limit our choice to our first impulse—that heat-of-the-moment reaction—which might not ultimately be the *best* choice. When we stop and take a breath, look at the situation from all angles, and weigh all our options, we are more likely to choose the response that will be most effective.

The overt expression of anger frequently leads to unintended consequences. When confronted with an angry communication, people—especially children—often respond to the anger, not the intended message. This is a conundrum. We usually express anger in the hopes of "clearing the air," of making a bad situation better. But reacting in anger often has exactly the opposite effect: anger is the emotion that usually makes a bad situation worse. (See "Anger Paradox Number One," page 87.)

Marlene and her mother, Phyllis, have a loving but contentious relationship. They often clash over minor matters, and the logistics of family holidays tends to be a hot-button issue. "No matter how hard I try to make a nice party, my mother always seems to find a way to mess things up," Marlene explained to me. "I don't know if she sees it as some kind of competition or power struggle or what. But she seems intent on sabotaging whatever I try to do."

One December, Marlene thought she had finalized plans to host the family at her home on Christmas Eve. But two weeks before the holiday, Phyllis left a message on her daughter's answering machine stating that she had decided she *had to* include a branch of aunts, uncles, and cousins in her own Christmas Eve plans, so she would visit Marlene on Christmas Day instead.

Marlene was furious. Not only was her mother being inconsiderate, but Marlene had also caught her in a lie. ("She had already told me that branch of the family was planning to be away!") Enraged, Marlene fired off an e-mail to her mother (with more than a touch of cyber-sarcasm) asking, "When did Aunt Rose and her family decide to stay home? Those were not the original plans."

Phyllis e-mailed back a defensive response, stating that Marlene was "clearly mistaken" and adding, "Since your house isn't big enough for all these additional relatives, I'll just have to entertain them myself."

Soon mother and daughter were not speaking on the phone, in person, or via Internet.

When Marlene explained her dilemma to me, we explored different ways she might proceed. I asked her, "What is your goal, not just for this event but for your relationship with your mother? And how do you think that goal might be achieved?" Now calmer, Marlene admitted that she just wanted to enjoy the holiday. She realized she wasn't about to change her mother's competitive hidden agenda (that was her mother's issue) but she could choose not to get caught up in the rivalry. And while Marlene might have wanted to righteously "stir things up" further— spreading word about her mother's manipulation of the facts and getting relatives to take sides—she realized this would not move her closer to her own goals.

Instead, Marlene decided to write a calmer e-mail to her mother. She explained that, while disappointed, she had to respect her mother's choice about whether or not to join Marlene's Christmas Eve party. However, Marlene firmly stated that she had her *own* plans for Christmas Day, rightfully asserting her autonomy.

Marlene got herself into a calmer mind-set before deciding how to respond to her mother's actions. That response not only reflected her own wishes and beliefs, but also set clear boundaries for their relationship— an appropriate "hiss!" But Marlene did not "bite back" by getting involved in pointless blaming or other tactics that would keep the anger level at fever pitch. The results here were not perfect, but they were a far cry from escalating a bad situation into one that would have been still worse.

This is a good place to tell you about one small amendment to upcoming Rule Number Four (breaking the family anger cycle begins with parents). That is surely true when dealing with your own children. But if you are dealing with your own angry parent, breaking the family anger cycle begins with the person who decides to be the mature adult.

Do Not Send E-Mail or Voice Mail in Anger!

Have you ever heard it said that when you are angry at someone, it might help to sit down and write them a letter . . . and then tear it up? The technique is designed to help you collect your thoughts, sharpen your focus, and hopefully process your rage in a harmless way. That's why the second part of the advice is to tear it up—or at the very least, put it away to revisit when you are in a calmer mood.

But since today's fast-paced world offers so many new communication options, this advice needs a bit of updating: if you do your writing on the computer, do not impulsively fire off that e-mail! E-mails sent in the heat of anger—or furious words left on an answering machine—leave tangible evidence. Days or even hours later, you will likely have simmered down. But that inflammatory message will be stored in someone's inbox or voice-mail system, ready to expose your rage with the click of a button.

For all its convenience, e-mail has another drawback: it doesn't allow you to see someone's facial expression or hear his or her tone of voice. Without these cues, it may be hard to detect whether a message has an underlying tone of humor, sarcasm, or something more insidious. In fact, some of the popular Internet abbreviations—LOL for *laughing out loud*, or the :) symbol to designate a smile—are designed to shed light on the sender's state of mind so misunderstandings won't develop.

I recall one patient who received a nasty e-mail from her sister: "Each time I reread it, I get furious all over again!" Reliving anger surely keeps it alive, and e-mail or voice-mail messages can be listened to again, saved, reread, printed, and archived. Think about *that* before you hit the send key or leave that message.

Rule Number Two

Do not buy into the myth that you will "explode" if you do not express your anger.

Now seriously: have you ever seen anyone literally explode with anger? It's quite an image! As explained in Chapter 2, the concept can be traced back to Pascal's hydraulic principle and Freud's original theories about the aggressive drive, suggesting that if rage is left unexpressed it will continue to build up, only to erupt at a potentially disastrous moment later on.

Patients often ask me if it is better to express anger directly or keep it contained; in other words, is expression or suppression the healthier way to go? There are also a host of important related questions: "What happens to anger when it is not expressed? Where does it go?" and "Does suppressed anger increase stress and contribute to disease?"

To look at the disease question first: while there does seem to be a widespread belief that unexpressed anger leads to illness, scientific data does not support that idea—at least not when it comes to cardiovascular disease. One landmark experiment conducted by Dr. Aaron Siegman, a psychologist at the University of Maryland, studied the cardiovascular reactivity hypothesis to see how "reliving" anger-provoking events might affect heart rate and blood pressure. Using a group of college student volunteers, Siegman examined the physiologic effects of re-experiencing anger under three different conditions: first, silently imagining a situation that made subjects angry; second, describing an anger-provoking event softly and slowly; and third, describing that same event in a loud and rapid voice. Under the first two conditions, subjects' heart rate and blood pressure hardly rose at all. But in the third scenario—which duplicated the kind of yelling and screaming associated with "expressing" anger—heart rate and blood pressure both went up. Siegman's study offered key evidence that simply *being angry* will not result in measurable increases in heart rate and blood pressure. It is how one manages anger—whether or not it is expressed in an overt way—that seems to produce physiologic changes that may eventually lead to illness.

Then there is the other extreme of anger expression: never let it show! In his tremendously popular book *The Road Less Traveled*, psychiatrist M. Scott Peck describes how hard it is to master the ideal of "[handling] our anger with full adequacy and competence." More often, he notes, we develop personal styles characterized by "the luxury of spontaneous anger" or "the safety of withheld anger."

While withheld anger can't be conclusively linked to disease, it can create a state of mind that mimics Pascal's hydraulic principle; that is, it may feel as if anger is slowly building up. If resentments accumulate over time and are never dealt with, even a trivial event can turn into the straw that broke the camel's back, causing an outburst that is out of proportion. While it may feel like the rage has been building up till it reaches the breaking point, the real problem is that the anger keeps getting reactivated. If some chronic, troubling, or unresolved issue pops up again and again, you will experience that same sense of rage each time it occurs.

Over the long term, continually swallowing anger is as ineffective as constantly venting it. You won't explode from holding your anger in, but it's likely that you won't find a way to effectively resolve it, either. Instead, the conditions underlying the anger must be processed, particularly in ongoing relationships.

Inevitably, there are good reasons for our anger. In his brilliant book *Anger*, the venerable Vietnamese Buddhist monk Thich Nhat Hanh suggests treating anger as "your baby." Instead of reacting in fury when you are angry, imagine your anger as your baby. Treat her with the sensitivity and gentleness that is required for her comfort and well-being. Admittedly, this is not easy when you are in the throes of rage, but thinking of your anger as a baby can be an extremely helpful thought when you are about to blast someone, thereby "throwing the baby out with the bathwater." Difficult relationship issues require patience and understanding.

Back to the first two points: *What happens to anger when it's not expressed?* and *Where does it end up?* This may sound startling, but when anger remains unexpressed . . . nothing happens to it. It doesn't go anywhere. There is no organ or other storage receptacle in our bodies for unexpressed anger.

Perhaps even more startling, once you forget about your anger, it does not exist. As long as you are no longer in contact with an anger-provoking stimulus, the anger simply *does not exist.* Indeed, if you are in a good mood and enjoying yourself, the anger you felt at the fellow who dangerously cut you off on the highway earlier in the day does not exist at all. That anger will be reactivated only if you think about the event. The thought then becomes the trigger, or stimulus, for re-experiencing the anger.

Rule Number Three

Accept that anger management is not easy; it has its ups and downs.

A play by Robert Anderson called *Double Solitaire* makes the following observation: "In every marriage more than two weeks old, there are grounds for divorce. The trick is to find, and continue to find, grounds for marriage." That bit of wisdom may well grow more true with each passing year—and become especially true when the marriage includes one or more children.

In a typical family, there is no shortage of good reasons to become angry. Many of us can tally thirty or more good reasons to lose our cool every day—wet towels on the floor, chores left undone, a blaring stereo, an abrupt remark, an unpaid bill. Along with these everyday stresses, there are also the deeper relationship issues that characterize family life: painful memories, rivalries, grudges, and so on.

But anger management is a process, not an overnight accomplishment. Even with the best intentions, there will be times when you will "lose it" and revert back to old patterns of behavior. Accept it and expect it. Even though I have been working with anger issues for several decades, on occasion I still fail at the task.

When you do fail, it is important not to then get angry at yourself for "losing it." Take a step back and have a chuckle. We *all* fail at anger management sometimes. Respect yourself for making the effort!

Carlos called himself a "typical grouch before coffee," defensively stating, "I've never been a morning person and my family just has to accept it!" Each day, as he and his wife, Isabel, faced the manic rituals of getting ready for work and getting two preschool sons off to day care, Carlos ranted and raved about everything—misplaced clothing, laundry left unfolded, a diaper bag that needed to be packed for their fifteen-month-old—each a potential anger trigger. Carlos's bad moods set a tone in the household and got everyone's day off to a bad start. Isabel complained that she reached work every morning with her stomach in a knot, while the two boys were beginning to become noticeably irritable themselves.

In therapy, Carlos admitted he had a few "issues" with the concept of putting the children in day care at such a young age—and expressed some guilt that his wife had to work so hard. Once he was able to face these issues directly and share some of his vulnerabilities with Isabel, the underlying tension between them was greatly reduced. Carlos saw that his "morning moods" were having a negative effect on the whole family, so we figured out some simple ways he might sidestep a few predictable triggers.

Since Carlos really *was* more energetic in the evening, he and Isabel took steps to assemble the children's clothes and other necessities the night before. He also set his alarm for twenty minutes earlier and had that

Anger Paradox Number One

An angry outburst usually makes it more difficult, not easier, to find a real solution.

When two people—especially two family members—are in conflict, they may think a good fight will clear the air and resolve the issue at hand. But it hardly ever happens; too often, the opposite is true. Anger tends to be contagious, and arguments can quickly erupt. And during arguments, everyone is far more concerned with proving her own point than with understanding someone else's! On and on it goes . . . and where it ends, no one knows.

Ironically, solutions may be even harder to come by after two (or more) people have argued. Arguments are rarely won or lost decisively, and the bad feelings they generate can last a very long time. Think about it: can you recall a time when you angrily criticized a parent, sibling, or child, only to have that relative reply, "Oh, I'm sorry! Thanks so much for pointing that out; I'll be sure not to do it again. Can you forgive me?" That may be a fantasy we all harbor, but it isn't likely to happen!

When people argue, they often respond to the other person's anger rather than the issue, even if it is critically important. One dysfunctional couple with a long history of verbal assaults was crossing a busy street. The woman was ahead of her husband, far out into the road, when he spotted a speeding car racing up the street. He shouted "Stop! Watch out!" at his wife, but she continued to walk across the street, apparently ignoring her husband's plea. The car narrowly missed the woman and she was shaken when her husband caught up to her. "Why didn't you listen to me?" he implored. "Because you were yelling at me!" the wife shot back. She could not hear her husband's important message because she reacted to his loud voice, which she perceived to be his characteristic anger.

needed cup of coffee as soon as he got out of bed. Carlos made a few more small changes in his morning routine—showering earlier so Isabel would have some extra time in the bathroom, and taking a twenty-minute run on the treadmill several days a week to help get him revved up. That way, he was able to meet the demands of the morning with more energy and a brighter outlook.

It's important to remember, again, that how we manage anger in adulthood is a matter of character. Some of us have a "characteristically" short fuse, so we are highly sensitive to the triggers we encounter. It can be worthwhile to take stock of what some of these triggers are in your own life and then, like Carlos, take some preventive measures to avoid them or minimize their impact.

Since you know yourself and your anger triggers better than anyone else does, you will be most able to determine what changes make sense. While many people initially react to this suggestion with "It can't be any different," upon further reflection virtually everyone I've worked with has found at least a few small changes that have made a big difference in the quality of their lives. Take a few moments to consider what triggers your anger most often.

Mood can greatly affect how we manage anger. When you are in generally good spirits, you can probably shrug off minor annoyances like heavy traffic, spilled soda, or a broken vending machine. But if you're overtired, pressed for time, preoccupied with financial worries—or all of the above—chances are you *will* be more vulnerable to the triggers around you. Many of us also have a shorter fuse at particular times, such as a pressing deadline, during an illness, or throughout the holidays.

And of course, moods can be particularly hard to hide in a family. If home is where we "let it all hang out," it stands to reason that family members get the full brunt of each other's crankiness. One unhappy result is that households can be an environment where turmoil is magnified. You aren't necessarily able to take a time-out or give yourself "breathing room" when you are having a problem with someone who lives under the same roof (maybe in the same room).

A vital part of anger management is simply knowing when your mood is apt to make you more reactive to particular triggers. For instance, if you've just walked in from a terrible day at work, you might say to your child, "Let's talk about the problems on your report card tomorrow morning; tonight, I'm a bit stressed out. I know I'll be calmer after a good sleep, and I'll be able to approach this with a clearer head." This kind of delaying tactic allows you to tackle the problem when you know you will be less prone to anger. (My wife and I have a pact that we *never* discuss difficult issues—especially money—after work in the evening; instead we choose morning or afternoon times, when we are both closer to our optimal functioning. I often recommend a similar strategy to my patients, and they report similarly good results.)

Anger Paradox Number Two

The ability to withhold anger is a sign of psychological strength, not weakness.

Sometimes the ability to express anger is mistakenly equated with psychological strength. Many people believe they will be perceived as ineffective if they don't get angry, citing aphorisms such as *The squeaky wheel gets the grease* and *Nice guys finish last*. Others fear they'll be dominated if they don't "stand up for themselves" by becoming indignant. Yet real psychological strength has to do with bringing a situation to a desired conclusion; it's not about blowing off steam. *Firmness of resolve* can be the best way to prevent domination. In the long run, knowing where you stand—and acting in accordance with that stance—will be more effective than initiating an outburst that typically amounts to impotent rage.

Anger can serve the crucial purpose of putting us in touch with our unfulfilled needs. But the paradox of expressing anger directly is that it typically reduces the likelihood that those needs will be fulfilled. As you will soon see, successful anger management means filling your needs. But when faced with your anger, others are not usually interested in being helpful with this process.

Rule Number Four

Breaking the family anger cycle begins with parents.

Since children learn many things by imitation, parents must be the ones to set a good example—particularly when it comes to establishing ground rules for how anger may and may not be displayed. As mothers and fathers, you are the leaders of your family. Children are the followers, the disciples. So whenever anger issues must be addressed in the family, realize that *you*, not your child, have to be the first to change.

When parents talk to me about a concern they have with a child—whether it's an anger-related issue or another kind of problem—they are often focused on ways to *get that child to alter her behavior.* Typically, when a child is behaving badly, mothers and fathers handle the situation in a particular way—such as screaming, threatening, or punishing—and if that tactic doesn't work, they often continue to scream, threaten, or punish with even more ferocity. As a result, the anger escalates and nothing gets resolved.

A father came to see me about problems he was having with his fourteen-year-old son. Since entering high school, Zachary had become increasingly surly and defiant, hanging out with the wrong crowd and sneaking out of the house at night; his grades were slipping as well. "I'm totally fed up with the kid!" the father told me in exasperation. "We told him he was grounded until his grades got better, and he just sneaks out behind our back. Then we told him if he ever pulled that stunt again, he's off the basketball team!" (Basketball was one of the few bright spots in Zachary's life, and he excelled on the court.) "I mean, what are we supposed to do? We're just gonna have to keep threatening until *something* gets through to him!"

Clearly, Zachary and his father were caught in a vicious cycle. The more Dad punished, the more Zachary defied; and the more Zachary defied, the more Dad punished. But while everyone grew angrier and angrier, Zachary's grades continued to be poor and his behavior was intolerable.

I assessed the situation with Zachary's father. "It seems that Zachary knows he'll be punished if he sneaks out of the house or disobeys other rules. Has that made him stop?"

The father admitted it hadn't, but then quickly went on: "If I don't show him who's boss, he'll get totally out of control!"

Again, I calmly tried to point out that this strategy only seemed to make matters worse.

"Then are you saying I should just let him get away with it, so he'll turn into a complete juvenile delinquent?!"

Hardly. When parents and children get locked into these anger-driven scenarios, parents have to make the first move. Often, it involves stepping back to take a calm, unemotional look at the situation and try to find ways to *reduce* rather than *intensify* the anger. We, the parents, have to change the way we act first.

Zachary's father realized that much of his own anger at his son was driven by fear: he was worried that Zachary was headed down the wrong path and might fall victim to problems with drugs or other harmful behaviors. Moreover, Zach's poor academic performance caused his father further alarm: how would he ever be able to get into a good college and get a good job?

I suggested to Zach's father that he spend some quality time with his son, without so much as mentioning these sensitive issues. One Sunday, they took a drive together and hit golf balls. The next week, Zach's father watched his son play basketball at the high school. To his father's amazement, Zach was the one who actually brought up the topic of his academic difficulties on the way home from the game. Zachary said that he was having a tough time with math and biology and acknowledged he was worried about being asked to leave the team.

Unable to share these fears before, Zachary had put up a mask of angry, defiant bravado; nobody was going to tell him what to do! But the bonding experience with his dad helped Zach realize his father was his advocate, not an adversary. Both father and son were then able to address the real issue at hand. In this case, the solution entailed getting Zach extra tutoring help so he could regain some mastery over his schoolwork. By bringing his own mounting anger to a halt, Zachary's father was able to really *help* his son instead

Anger Paradox Number Three

Anger often gives you *less*, not more, control over a situation.

One intended purpose of expressing anger is to gain greater control over a situation—either by making your feelings known or by getting someone else to accede to your wishes. Yet, paradoxically, an angry outcry often *reduces* your control—since it puts you *at the mercy of someone else's reaction*. Inflict your anger and the other party may fight back directly, spread nasty rumors to other family members, or retaliate in a hundred other ways. Results can be very far from what you expected.

A Chinese proverb says, "Once anger leaves your lips, you are no longer its master." When we get angry or criticize someone, there is often an accompanying wish to make that someone more aware of how their behavior is affecting us, so they will change their behavior. But criticism delivered in anger is rarely perceived as constructive. Instead of greater awareness, we will likely engender greater resentment. And that's a lose-lose proposition.

of engaging in a standoff with him. It turned things around, transforming a lose-lose situation into one in which everyone emerged a winner.

Rule Number Five

Do not threaten separation or abandonment when you are angry.

The old adage about sticks and stones breaking bones is only partly true: they do break bones, but they aren't the only weapons that inflict irreparable pain. Words said in anger can cut deep and wound badly. There are a few anger management rules that are, figuratively speaking, engraved in stone (in the same way that the "bite" in the swami fable is indisputably verboten). Physical violence is off-limits. Likewise, threats of abandonment or separation should not be considered a valid strategy for managing angry feelings.

The fear of abandonment is one of the most primal fears we humans ever experience. It originates very early in life, at a time when a child is fully dependent on parents or caregivers for her very survival. Imagine the terror of a young child who believes that she will not have parents to rely on for support; she surely feels vulnerable and afraid. If parents reactivate that fear during moments of intense anger, it can be extremely damaging to a child's sense of security.

If you are angry at your child, spouse, or anyone else, do not say, "I can't stand to live with you anymore. You're not my daughter," or something similar. In such circumstances, it is almost always impossible for the "rejectee" to process the information directed her way; the feelings of abandonment are just too overwhelming. Threats of abandonment strike at the core of a person's existence, often instilling terror at the thought of being left alone.

Have an arsenal of emergency anger management strategies to tap into during times when you feel yourself coming close to the "abandonment" threat. As former president Thomas Jefferson once said, "If angry count to ten, if very angry count to one hundred." Go for a walk. Take a bath. Go to a movie. In short, do whatever it takes to remove yourself from the anger-provoking scenario, so you won't say something impulsive and furious that you may deeply regret later.

A quote from Robert Fulghum's *Everything I Need to Know I Learned in Kindergarten* states, "Sticks and stones will break our bones, but anger breaks our hearts." A crucial aspect of anger management is understanding when, why, and how you may have to take yourself out of the situation so you will have a chance to reflect on how best to respond (not simply react) to the anger-provoking stimuli around you.

Dr. Allan's Anger Management Formula will give you a constructive, workable plan for anger management. These are guidelines to help you navigate typical scenarios, in and out of the family, with constructive advice about what to do, what not to do, and when to distance yourself from an escalating emotional climate. Now it's time to learn about a powerful metaphor for managing anger: the *hook*. It's the next step in breaking an insidious generational anger cycle.

Step One:
Identify the Hook

Take a few moments to try this visualization exercise. Close your eyes and think back to a time when you were *really* angry. Now try to picture that anger as a literal, physical thing. What does it look like? How can it increase? How might it be stored? What would need to happen to make it diminish or disappear?

When most of us visualize our anger in this way, chances are we seize on some variation of the aggressive drive, the hydraulic principle, or both. Most likely, we envision our anger as a growing thing, something that gets larger and larger within the confines of a small, closed space—similar to steam or water building up within a narrow pipe or lava about to erupt from a seething volcano. As anger builds, it becomes more intense; we might think of ourselves "reaching the boiling point." We express the need to vent—that is, discharge some anger by "blowing off steam" or getting it out of our system. Perhaps, like Joan in Chapter 2, we may worry that we will "explode" if that anger isn't released.

Yet this understanding of anger is highly inaccurate. Believe it and you will most likely engage in self-defeating ways of managing your anger. You will almost always become frustrated despite your best intentions of managing your anger constructively.

Now I will show you how to visualize your anger in a new and altogether different way.

Imagine yourself navigating through the "sea of life" in much the same way a fish swims through water. You are venturing along peacefully when suddenly a hook, with a tasty-looking bait on it, drops in front of you. This hook is anything that could potentially make you angry for a *good reason*: poor service, an exasperating telephone menu, slow drivers in the passing lane, someone who doesn't say thank you when you hold the door—all of these things qualify. Some hooks are more personal: a mean remark from your neighbor, a party to which you didn't get invited, a colleague who slacks off at work yet always manages to get more than his share of credit. And then there are the innumerable things waiting to hook you in your everyday family life: clothes left on the floor, an exorbitant bill, an oil burner that breaks down in twenty-degree weather, a spouse's demand that you go out and rake leaves when you planned to relax with a good book.

To return to the fish-in-the-sea metaphor, imagine that you find yourself swimming along when there it is, a hook with some delicious bait on it—that is, a really good reason to get angry.

Understanding What Hooks You

The hook is a powerful symbol for how we react to anger-provoking situations. The hook metaphor has a historic origin. It was developed by Dr. Lynda H. Powell for the Recurrent Coronary Prevention Project

Figure 5.1

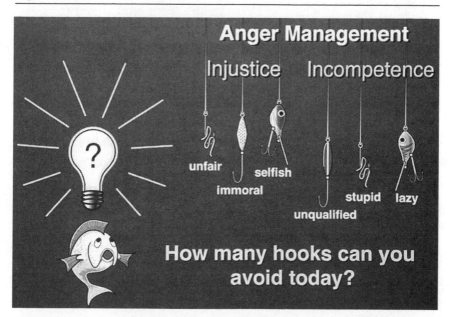

Source: Courtesy of Lynda H. Powell, "The Hook: A Metaphor for Gaining Control of Emotional Reactivity," in *Heart & Mind*, Robert Allan and Stephen Scheidt, eds. Washington, DC: American Psychological Association, 1996.

(RCPP), a landmark 1986 study to help post–heart attack patients reduce their chronic cardiovascular reactivity. The RCPP enrolled individuals who had suffered a heart attack and divided them into two groups. The first received standard post–heart attack counseling, including discussions about the importance of diet, exercise, and proper medication in avoiding future cardiac events (such as heart attacks, angioplasty, and coronary bypass surgery).

The second group—the intervention group—received this same education and something more: cognitive-behavioral psychotherapy to help alter their own personal anger and many of the beliefs associated with type A behavior. Participants were challenged to rethink their beliefs about material achievement, self-esteem, the need for approval, and the importance of being in control. At the same time, they were offered concise anger management techniques—including training in how to use the hook metaphor—to get a clearer picture of how anger is triggered and how it can be better managed. Second heart attack rates were reduced by 44 percent for those in the intervention group compared to the control group. Participants in the RCPP rated the hook as the single most valuable tool they had encountered in their treatment. Indeed, in my own life and practice, the hook has helped to reduce anger and provide me with greater freedom of choice.

Each time we get angry we trigger our fight-or-flight response, which not only boosts heart rate and blood pressure but also releases "sticky" platelets into the bloodstream. For that reason, anger issues can be particularly hazardous to cardiac patients, many of whom take an aspirin each day in order to keep their platelets flowing smoothly.

Platelets form blood clots, which can be lifesaving if you cut yourself shaving. People with clotting disorders, such as hemophilia, can bleed to death if they have even a small cut. However, most heart attacks and certain kinds of strokes occur when a plaque in an artery ruptures and a clot forms on top of the ruptured plaque, creating a situation much like a dam. Blood cannot flow downstream past the blockage, and the heart (or brain) becomes deprived of the life-sustaining oxygen that is dissolved in the blood.

Indeed, we know that about 1.3 percent of non-fatal heart attacks, approximately thirteen thousand a year in the United States, are triggered by intense anger. Understanding how we get hooked by valid reasons to get angry—in other words, being able to picture the process in a different way—has helped many patients to see that they had more than one response option. They were no longer at the mercy of their first angry impulses.

While there will always be a temptation to meet an anger-provoking situation with justifiable rage, we can choose not to react, not to bite the hook. And one key aspect of anger management is learning how to recognize and avoid the many hooks that will inevitably "drop down" in front of you.

The Two "I" Hooks: Injustice and Incompetence

Think about all the hooks you typically encounter—all the attractive lures for anger—and you will find that most fall into two categories, the two "I"s: *injustice* and *incompetence*. We have a tendency to "bite," or get angry, whenever we encounter a circumstance that we perceive as unfair or a situation that puts us at the mercy of someone or something inept.

The fairness question is a deeply rooted part of the human condition. Carol Tavris, one of the foremost authorities on anger, believes there is a universal human sense of justice: "Life is not a fair game . . . but people have a curious capacity to behave as if it were. We tend to equate what is with what ought to be, and react with outrage to attacks on our way of doing things." We are apt to feel profoundly disappointed, frustrated, and angry when things are not how we believe they should be. Virtually all social movements begin with anger at some condition that is deemed by many individuals to be unfair.

Ironically, unfairness is as much a part of the human condition as our wish for life to be fair. A lucky few enjoy what some may deem to be unfair advantages, like inherited wealth, power, beauty, genius, or great talent. The rest of us are relegated to hard work and limited opportunities. Still others have the unduly harsh burdens of illness, poverty, and other hardships that are often beyond their control. Injustice is all around us.

Life is also full of those niggling injustices that rub us all the wrong way. It's unfair that we are herded onto overcrowded freeways or face delays on public transportation, that politicians we've elected ignore our concerns and pursue their own agendas, that HMOs deny us coverage after we've paid handsomely for their premiums. These are just a tiny fraction of the inequities we endure as part of daily functioning in the modern world.

Then there is the second category of anger triggers that are so rampant in modern life: incompetence. A technician repairs your computer but it stops working again ten minutes after he's out the door; a repairman takes your money yet still hasn't fixed that ping in the dishwasher. A coworker misplaces a vital client's phone number. A waiter brings the wrong order; the chef cooks your food well-done instead of rare. The list goes on and on.

Family life also provides plenty of reason to label our nearest and dearest incompetent. We can easily become irritated with children who fail to complete their homework or a spouse who neglects to make an entry in the checkbook. How many wives have fumed at an overly confident husband who frequently gets lost, yet refuses to ask for directions? Not putting tools away, leaving the house without sufficient time to make the train or bus . . . even that old saw about leaving the cap off the toothpaste can be sufficient grounds for an argument. The small, inevitable annoyances of daily living tend to be spotlighted and even magnified on the home front. As a result, it becomes all too easy to find evidence of incompetence everywhere you look.

Yet each time we get angry, we risk getting hooked by one of these annoyances. Even worse, biting a hook can result in getting "pulled out of the water," a situation with the potential to become much more perilous. It is roughly comparable to losing our freedom: we become slaves to our impulses and limit our choices to our initial reaction. As a result, we forfeit the opportunity to consider the long-term consequences of our behavior. Whenever we get hooked by an anger-provoking situation, we can find ourselves feeling, metaphorically speaking, like a fish out of water.

It is common to believe that anger has a life of its own, that you have no choice but to express your anger or face dire consequences. But you can control and manage anger much less destructively when you realize that you don't have to bite the hook! Instead, you can recognize that while you do see a tasty-looking bait—a justifiable reason to get angry over some blatant display of injustice or incompetence—danger lurks beneath in the form of a hook. And you can

Hooks Wherever You Look!

Think about some of the things that make you angry. Chances are you can get hooked whenever you come up against injustice or incompetence—and these bothersome experiences tend to come in many forms.

Injustice describes all those situations or the behaviors of others that are:

Unfair
Immoral
Improper
Wrong
Selfish
Inconsiderate
Biased
"Bad"

Incompetence covers any action we perceive as:

Inept
Incapable
Inadequate
Unqualified
Stupid
Lazy

choose to swim on by. When you have your first success with this technique you will be wonderfully
empowered, as you make a more effective choice.

Learning How to Spot Your Hooks

Gail is the single mother of a twelve-year-old daughter, Janie. To hear her tell it, she is a woman who has
not caught too many breaks in life—and an outsider
would be likely to agree. Gail grew up with an angry,
alcoholic father and a mother who suffered off and on
from clinical depression. As the oldest of three children, Gail not only shouldered more than her share of
responsibility—cooking and cleaning whenever her
mother was bedridden, and often staying home to
babysit for her younger brother and sister—but she
was a ready target for her father's drunken rages. "He
was a man who had worked hard to put himself
through school, and then showed a lot of early promise as a mechanical engineer," Gail recalls. "But with
all the pressure of work and supporting a family, he
began to drink more heavily. There were lots of job
losses and lots of fighting at home." Early on, Gail
learned to cope by taking on the responsible role. She
became a top student, winning scholarships to put herself through college. College offered Gail the opportunity to visualize her life in more positive terms, as
she got a healthy taste of independence and worked
toward a degree in education.

College was also where Gail met her future husband, Bill. At first, she was attracted by his carefree, dynamic personality. "He seemed like such a free spirit, so different from me," she recalls. They married shortly after graduation, and their daughter Janie was born two years later. Yet within a few years, things began to sour. Bill's "free spirit" gradually turned into a pattern of reckless, irresponsible behavior. As his use of illegal drugs escalated, he put the young family into serious debt. He jumped from job to job and became increasingly hostile to Gail, who by now was the household's sole breadwinner and the one who held everything together, much as she had in her family growing up.

By the time I met Gail, she had left the marriage. But the stress of being a single mother was becoming overwhelming. Gail loved Janie and wanted her to have a happy, promising future. At the same time, she had begun to aim more and more of her own rage at her daughter—the closest available target—and she knew she wanted that to stop.

In therapy, Gail spoke of how bitter and angry she felt about the way her life had turned out. "Why am I the one always left holding the bag?" she cried. Gail's painful history left her particularly vulnerable to getting hooked by any situation she perceived as unfair—whether it was getting stuck with her husband's debts (a major injustice) or being forced to pick up Janie's carelessly strewn clothes (a minor irritation).

I suggested that Gail get a small notebook to keep with her at all times. In the course of a day, whenever she found herself getting angry, she should take a moment to jot down a brief description of the events that annoyed her. At first Gail was skeptical, but she was willing to give the exercise a try.

For several days, Gail made note of every anger-provoking incident. A parent-teacher conference called at the last minute. A parking ticket received just minutes after the meter ran out. News that her former sister-in-law was criticizing Gail's mothering skills behind her back. ("And she doesn't have a clue about what I went through with her brother!") Discovering that Janie had used more than her allotment of cell phone minutes triggered Gail's wrath as well.

Soon Gail began to recognize a pattern: she really *did* seem to react strongly to any circumstance she deemed unjust, especially when she felt she was asked to contribute more than her fair share. Once she learned to recognize those injustice hooks—and realize her own overwhelming tendency to bite them whenever they dropped in front of her—she was able to step back and see things more objectively. If she started becoming inflamed over, say, an extra work responsibility or Janie's unmade bed, she learned to stop and say *hook!* And she gradually trained herself not to bite it, but to swim on by: in other words, to avoid the hook and find a constructive way to address the relevant issue or problem.

How to Swim On By

From my personal experience, I know the hook can be a powerful tool for reducing unwanted anger. Here is how to put the concept into practice:

1. Begin a "Hook Book," a small notebook that can be easily carried in a pocket or handbag. Jot down notes about each time you are provoked and get angry. Set up the pages as follows:

    Anger Event   Hook

    For example, under the Anger Event heading, you might write "Husband watching TV when the house is so messy." Figure out why that situation is a hook for you and write that under the Hook heading, for example, "Unfair that he doesn't do his share of cleaning" or "Unfair that he's relaxing while I'm working." Keep descriptions brief and to the point. Be sure to carry the book with you, and try to jot down your descriptions immediately after the event happens.

2. After several days, or up to a week if you haven't had many anger-provoking experi-

ences, review your Hook Book. Look for recur-
ring themes—particular circumstances, places,
times of day, and so on. On a separate page,
record the themes that occurred more than
three times. For each theme, describe:

Who was involved?
How did you feel?
How did you react?
What was your "hook"?

3. Review the themes closely—these are some of
your anger hooks. Next to each event, add a
note about whether the hook can be characterized as an *injustice* or an *incompetence*.
These designations will help you avoid biting
into future hooks.

The Value of a Hook Book

In counseling patients, I find that the Hook Book is a
very constructive tool. By having the book with you
at all times, you will be better able to describe your
reactions as they happen, rather than trying to recap-
ture that same emotional mind-set hours or days later.

Just as a diary can be a revelation of your inner
thoughts, a Hook Book serves as a blueprint of your
anger. How many times do you typically get angry in

the course of a day? What kinds of things hook you? Do you usually encounter a batch of small hooks (minor annoyances), or a few overwhelming big hooks (major issues)? By studying what is on the page, you may suddenly see particular themes or patterns you never spotted before. It's quite likely that you will gain a better understanding of what makes you angry. And becoming alert to those issues may very well help you avoid biting into future hooks.

Spotting the Small Hooks

You will probably notice that much of your anger is elicited by minor, ephemeral events: traffic jams, slow service in restaurants, not getting a seat on the train, an irritating remark from a coworker, or a dirty look from a stranger. These are typically the kinds of things that are most easily managed by first identifying and then avoiding the hook. For instance, if you find yourself becoming hot under the collar when confronting a surly waiter or when you are stuck in a slow-moving line, say to yourself, *hook*—and you may well be able to avoid biting into it.

This is what Gail was able to do as she confronted some of the minor problems in her own Hook Book. "I noticed that for three days running, I blew up at Janie in the evening when I was overtired and still had papers to correct," she said. "It was always over something minor: one night she needed poster board for a school project and didn't tell me till the last minute, and the next night she finished up all the shampoo. But each time I totally lost it."

Upon further reflection, Gail also recalled that evening was a particularly troubling time of day when she was growing up, since it was when her father was most likely to be drunk and abusive. She gradually came to see that the combination of present stresses and past memories made her more apt to get hooked at this time of day—ironically, a time when she most looked forward to connecting with Janie. "Seeing it in black and white in a notebook really helped me spot the pattern," Gail notes. "I can't say I'm perfect, but I know where the hooks are now. And I'm getting a lot better at avoiding them."

When you are first creating a Hook Book, it helps to make note of relevant details, such as times, places, or people you happen to be with when your anger gets the best of you. Then if there is a pattern, as there was with Gail, you are apt to spot it more easily.

I recall another patient, Frank, who was part of a support group I was leading. Frank was very "type A"—a hard-driving attorney with little patience when things didn't go his way. Not surprisingly, given his profession and temperament, Frank had considerable difficulty with incompetence hooks. He yelled at subordinates who made minor errors and berated his two teenage sons if they failed to make straight As.

But in his late forties, Frank suffered a heart attack. He decided he had better adopt a more effective way of managing his anger if he hoped to live at all. In this respect, his determination served him well. Frank became a committed member of a support group for cardiac patients. He easily adopted many of the lifestyle measures, such as healthier eating and regular exercise, with characteristic passion.

Anger management was a more arduous challenge, however. Frank needed to take stock of his hooks, particularly those related to others' competence and performance. Sometimes in the support group he would begin to grow noticeably agitated if his fellow members took up too much time or had difficulty getting a point across. Then he came to realize these were hooks—so rather than bite, he learned to remind himself that others had the same right as he did to be heard and respected. He also reminded himself that some of the other group members were not as verbally skilled as he was, and he became more tolerant of their more limited communication expertise. After all, Frank was an attorney, someone who earned a handsome living in part because of his considerable talents as a wordsmith.

One day, about a year after his heart attack, Frank proudly shared a story with the group that showed just how far he had come in managing his incompetence hooks. "I brought my car to the dealer for routine service," he explained. "I picked it up and proceeded to drive all of three blocks, when the right front wheel fell off!" Fortunately, Frank was driving quite slowly at the time (which represented another milestone in his overall plan to take things easier), but the experience was nonetheless frightening and anger-provoking. As he walked back to the dealer, Frank could feel his rage at the incompetent mechanic start to overtake him: "What kind of moron would forget to tighten the lug nuts on the wheels?"

But as he heard these thoughts running through his head, Frank recognized the situation for what it was: a hook. He could be his old hothead self and storm into the dealership with screams and threats; or he could choose not to bite the hook, but instead to handle the situation with a calmer tactical strategy.

Choosing the second option, Frank composed himself. He went in to speak to the manager and (more or less) quietly described what happened. "They couldn't have been more attentive," Frank recalled. "The manager apologized profusely and not only fixed the problem immediately, but even gave me a sizable refund on the repair bill." The support group applauded Frank and gave him further validation for his wise decision.

Then one member made an interesting point: in such situations people often get hooked by imagining what *might have happened* rather than recognizing what did. Suppose Frank had been seriously injured by the mechanic's negligence, losing a wheel while driving sixty miles per hour on the freeway? It's not only a terrifying scenario but a real possibility.

But fortunately, this particular incident did not have grave consequences; both Frank and the car emerged virtually unscathed. And while these worst-case scenarios may be valid possibilities, envisioning them doesn't do us much good; it usually only produces an endless string of "what-if" worries that make it more difficult, not easier, to manage our anger. In short, it makes the bait on the hook appear more and more appealing.

Tackling the Major Hooks

Not all hooks can be classified as everyday annoyances, of course. As you look over the entries in your own Hook Book, chances are that you will see some bigger issues come into focus. Just as Gail realized she was apt to be hooked by demonstrations of injustice—and that her painfully unfair life trajectory was a big reason for that—you too might be able to see a link between your own early formative experiences of emotional pain, deprivation, or other hardships and the things that really make you angry today. Such awareness may make it easier to spot predictable, recurrent hooks in your life.

Frank may have been skillful at sidestepping conflicts with his mechanic, but he had deeper issues in his relationships with his two sons—Josh, age seventeen, and Alex, age fourteen. Josh was a semi-serious student with his own anger streak; he resented his father's frequent hounding about the need to "get better grades and make something of yourself, like I did!" Alex, by contrast, was a gregarious young man whose talents centered more on theater and music than academics. Frank had anger problems with them both.

Too Hot to Cool Down?

Why is it so difficult to cool down after you get
angry? Research done on animals points to the
amygdala, a primitive structure in the brain. This
tiny almond-shaped organ coordinates the body's
autonomic and endocrine systems and is responsible for the fight-or-flight response that enabled
our ancestors to survive.

Anger also stimulates the amygdala—and
once stimulated, it takes awhile for the amygdala
to return to its resting state. For instance, when
hungry dogs observe other dogs eating, it's usually more than an hour before the physiologic
effects (salivating, increased secretion of gastric
juices, and so on) disappear. In a similar way,
when people feel angry, it often takes some time
to calm down; anger's aftereffects don't wear off
instantly. Scientists believe this is probably rooted
in basic survival: whatever threat you confronted
may still be nearby, so it helps to have that
heightened response around for a while. But from
an anger management perspective, these lingering aftereffects can be troublesome since they
may increase the likelihood that, once angry, you
will more easily get angry again. That's another
reason it's better not to bite the hook in the first
place.

"Josh has a lot of potential, but he wastes it all and he's got that damn chip on his shoulder. If I ever gave my father the kind of disrespect he gives me, I'd get a smack across the face," Frank complained. "And Alex spends much too much time partying. Plus he's got to get that acting business out of his head, or he'll never amount to anything!" Frank believed his own high standards would serve as an inspiration to his sons. However, he was merely making them feel browbeaten and intimidated.

Frank's heart attack had serious repercussions for this family. No longer the indestructible patriarch, he was forced to show a more vulnerable side to his two children. In turn, the entire family—including Frank's wife, Beth, who had always taken a passive role in her children's upbringing and deferred to her husband's dictatorial ways—needed to reexamine their rigid belief system. "I came to realize I was putting too much pressure on Josh and Alex, just as my father had pressured me," Frank explained. "My father lost his father at a very young age, so he had to quit school and contribute to the family's support. He was determined that I would have the opportunities he never did— that I would be the success he never could be—and he became enraged anytime I seemed to be slacking off."

Haunted by the specter of *not* being prosperous (a fear that resonated in Frank's childhood home, since it had shaped his father's bitter outlook on life), Frank took pains not to show any weakness to his sons and never to tolerate anything less than perfection. He gradually saw that this stance not only alienated his children, it trampled on their freedom to pursue their own life goals. Frank also came to understand why incompetence hooks were such an anger trigger for him. "All my life, I've been made to feel that being less than perfect is unacceptable," Frank recalled. "So anytime my sons didn't seem to be living up to my standards, it made me go ballistic. I felt like a bad parent: I believed a good father would have sons who wanted to be just like him." Despite the anger issues, Frank also had great love for his sons, along with a willingness to confront and amend his own mistakes.

What Happens If You Do Get Hooked?

By now, you may imagine that despite your best efforts, you will still continue to occasionally get hooked. You will! One key aspect of anger management is recognizing that it's impossible *not* to have some setbacks.

So what happens when you do get hooked? What if, despite your best efforts, you find yourself taking the bait and getting angry at the slipshod repairman, the crashed computer, or the uncooperative child? Try to get the hook "out of your mouth" as quickly as possible! Count to ten. Take some deep breaths. Treat yourself the same way you would treat a three-year-old and give yourself a time-out, perhaps by going to a favorite chair or taking a few minutes to zone out in front of the TV.

In short, give yourself a chance to disengage from the hook so you can regain a calmer demeanor and a clearer perspective. From there, it's easier to figure out your most effective response. You might remember my all-time favorite quote about anger, from Montaigne: "Things truly seem different to us once we have quieted and cooled down."

Frank's mishap with the car had one unintended benefit. It forced him to take a walk, which is one effective way to defuse anger. Walking not only takes you to a different place—putting space between you and the hook, as it were—but it requires you to exert some physical effort. That allows your stress hormones to be metabolized as you move your muscles and engage in a healthy cardiovascular workout. This way the stress hormones are not circulating freely through your bloodstream, possibly contributing to the process of damaging your arteries.

Being able to navigate our way around all these hooks gives us more power. Sometimes the trick lies in spotting the hook in advance and figuring out a way to swim aside: for example, steering clear of a combative coworker or deliberately *not* talking politics with your father-in-law. Other times, the hooks are unavoidable—a flat tire, a short-tempered spouse, a teenager who hurls a nasty remark your way . . . such things can catch you by surprise. When unexpected hooks appear, it's important to recognize each as a hook and make an effort not to bite—regardless of how tasty the bait might appear.

This strategy will give you greater mastery over your environment. You will no longer be controlled by myriad annoyances: traffic jams, inept mechanics, and unresolved minor conflicts. You can choose how to *respond*, rather than *react*, to these stressors.

Anger management is generally a three-step process. Spotting the hooks is Step One. Understanding which *need* is being frustrated is Step Two. *Filling that need* is Step Three.

Three Steps to Managing Anger

1. Identify your hook. But don't bite it! Do *not* express your anger.
2. Identify which of your *needs* is not being met (respect? territory?).
3. Fill your need, or adjust to the fact that you can't.

Now that you know how to spot a hook—Step One—the next two chapters will tackle Steps Two and Three, helping you understand how to recognize and effectively deal with your unmet needs.

Step Two:
Identify the Need

To tackle this next exercise, dig out your Hook
Book once again.

Open to any page. At random, select one of the
anger events you wrote down. Or, if you haven't yet
started a Hook Book, take a few moments to designate and describe any event in the past week that
made you very angry, or hooked you—indicating
whether the experience could be designated as an
injustice hook, an incompetence hook, or both. If you
discover that you are getting hooked *again* by review-
ing the event, take a deep breath and say to yourself,
"Oh well . . . "

Suppose the event in question centers on a work
project. One afternoon, you are sitting at your desk
when you receive a frantic phone call from a department manager: "Can you have a PowerPoint presen-

tation ready for an important meeting in forty minutes?" The request entails canvassing your computer to find the relevant facts and figures, all for a client meeting you are just hearing about *this very minute*. It isn't even your client—or your meeting—but the manager in question is a superior who could easily shift the blame to you if things don't work out. And although you should have received adequate advance notice, the manager seems to quickly gloss over that point and expect it will be done in the unreasonable amount of time allotted. In short, you're in the hot seat, and you had better find a solution fast.

Of course, your own anger incident may bear no resemblance to this hypothetical example—perhaps it was a family fight or a random confrontation with a stranger—but a central principle of anger management is that anger occurs when a *need* is frustrated. Beyond basic needs for food, clothing, and shelter, the needs most frequently embedded in anger-provoking situations can be broadly grouped into two categories:

1. Respect and a desire to be understood
2. Territory, either physical or psychological

Most of the time we are unaware that one or both of these important needs have been frustrated when we become angry. As you remember whatever occurrence had you seething—making you mind-blind with rage—ask yourself this elemental question: *Was one of these two needs violated? Did I become angry because someone or something failed to show me the respect I rightfully deserve? Did they understand what I was trying to communicate? Was there some encroachment on my territory, my turf, my personal space? Were both of these important needs challenged?*

Respect and Understanding

Back in the '60s, Aretha Franklin's "Respect" became a popular anthem that tapped into a universal human need: "R-E-S-P-E-C-T . . . All I'm askin' for is a little respect." Today's young people speak scornfully of being "dissed," a shorthand street term for *disrespected.* Among adolescents (of any age), getting dissed can be grounds for a serious altercation.

When a person feels dissed, he usually expresses an angry concern that someone else's actions have left him feeling *slighted* (another interesting word, since it equates so strongly to being trivialized or made to feel unimportant). At heart, that is what disrespect is all about. And it comes in many forms: when someone fails to signal when changing lanes, or cuts ahead of you in line, or divulges something you shared in confidence, or doesn't return money you lent—these are all forms of disrespect, and any one of them can make us very angry.

I remember an incident with one patient, Jim, that was a typical "disrespect scenario." Jim was in a cardiac rehab program and had just finished using six of the seven exercise machines in his standard workout.

As he approached the last machine, he noticed that someone else was idly perched on it, enjoying a casual conversation. When Jim asked if he could use this piece of equipment he was met with an abrupt, "Can't you use something else?" He explained that he had completed his workout except for this last machine. But the "squatter" made no attempt to end his conversation or relinquish the equipment.

This is a prime example of an injustice hook. It was grossly unjust (or unfair, in popular parlance) that Jim was denied access to equipment he needed, when it would have been easy for the offending party to simply get up and continue his conversation in another spot. Moreover, Jim had paid a fee to the rehab program, so he was justified in assuming he would have reasonable access to its resources. The equipment was part of the "turf" Jim had paid for. This is one of those scenarios where the needs for both respect *and* territory had been violated.

Did Jim have a right to be angry? Absolutely! He said he felt like blurting out, "You're not even *using* that equipment and I need it. Get the #$% out of my way!" But would this have led to a successful resolution? Not likely. Even if Jim had the momentary victory of claiming the machine, he would have made an enemy.

You might be thinking, *so what?* But think a bit further. This solution would have led to bad feelings each time Jim ran into the individual in the rehab facility. Perhaps the conflict might have escalated, as Jim and the machine squatter would have exchanged dirty looks every time each of them tried to assert his right to use the equipment. The stranger could have become a real anger hook for Jim, causing him to relive his fury each time the two came in contact. If that anger had been expressed directly, it's likely both men would have been upset for some time afterward—and for cardiac patients, anger can be a dangerous matter.

It would have been valuable for Jim to *consciously realize* that he was angry because he was being treated with disrespect. Moreover, it was his adversary—not Jim—who had the problem and was behaving badly. In such circumstances we typically feel a flash of rage without truly processing its source: being the brunt of someone's disrespect.

If Jim had tapped into his own need to be treated with respect, rather than his desire to "even the score," he might have seized on a number of creative ways to handle things with his rehab adversary. As it was, Jim skipped that last piece of equipment and left the center frustrated and angry; that's why he reported the incident in his next therapy session. Jim had previously been something of a hothead and was now fearful his anger might get out of control, boosting his risk of a heart attack. We spent a number of sessions discussing ways Jim might be assertive without being aggressive. Learning how to spot his own hooks was a vital first step.

Just as it's helpful to spot an anger hook for what it is, it is important to recognize that accompanying

Managing Your Anger Can Save Your Life

Research shows that about 1.3 percent of heart attacks, and likely a similar percentage of sudden cardiac deaths, are triggered by intense anger. Most heart attacks occur when a blood clot, formed by "sticky" platelets, clump together on top of a plaque that has ruptured. This blocks the flow of blood in much the same way that a dam keeps water from flowing downstream, resulting in the death of heart tissue, a *myocardial infarction*—in popular terms known as a heart attack. It is believed that in response to intense anger, coronary arteries sometimes undergo *vasoconstriction*, or spasm. In such circumstances, the spasm can rupture a plaque, ultimately triggering a heart attack. That's one more reason it pays to manage anger: it may prolong your life!

each hook there is an unmet need. So rather than taking the bait and biting the hook, the best strategy is to figure out a way to fill the need. If you can identify the fact that a particular interaction is making you feel "dissed," and then deal directly with the need for respect, anger can be better managed.

How else might Jim have dealt with this situation? He could have quietly stood his ground; perhaps the other person would have slowly gotten the message. Or he could have calmly asked, "How long are you going to be?" Jim might have opted to leave the scene for a few moments, perhaps saying, "Could you save my turn?" Or he might have told the machine loiterer, "Sorry, I'm in a bit of a rush; I have an important appointment. Could you help me out?" Jim and I discussed these options, and he realized he now had smarter coping strategies in case he ever encountered such a situation again.

The best course for Jim in the future would be to figure out how to get his own need met—the emotional need for respect as well as the practical need to use the machine (the territory in question). Biting the hook by getting angry at the provocateur won't accomplish either of these goals without undesirable consequences.

Negotiating Family Matters

Of course, many of the respect issues between parents and children are more complex than Jim's chance interaction at the gym. Not surprisingly, it can also be more challenging to fulfill unmet needs in the difficult interactions we have with family members.

Claire and her husband, Al, have always had a turbulent relationship with Al's mother, Harriet. "She's been a domineering pain in the neck for as long as I've known her!" fumes Claire, citing a span of time that covers Claire and Al's twenty-two-year marriage.

Lack of Respect and Understanding: Angry Situations Prompted by Disrespect

Disrespect comes in many forms, guises, and disguises. Any one of the following can be a hook to make you angry:

- Verbal abuse (angry, sarcastic, threatening, condescending, or obscene language)
- Disparaging remarks made about you, your family, or your friends
- Lying
- Failing to keep a promise
- Comparing you unfavorably to another
- Imposing another person's values on you
- Making decisions for you, or doing something that affects you, without first getting your permission
- Threatening or carrying out violence

Throughout his childhood years, Al saw his mother as a strict, formidable figure—someone who bullied her family into submission with a combination of angry outbursts and sharp criticism. Al was the second youngest of five children, a convivial son who developed a pattern of passive, compliant responses to his mother's demands. Al's father, Ralph, was a quiet man who spent long hours in the workplace. He would occasionally sympathize with Al and his siblings, but his was a kind of "peace-at-any-price" stance: "What can I do? It doesn't pay to argue with her." Both his words and his actions conveyed the message to his children that giving Harriet exactly what she wanted was the safest way to go.

"It's fair to say that in our house, it was my mother's way or *no* way," Al says ruefully. Not surprisingly, Harriet was also the only member of the family who routinely expressed anger. Her husband and children may have seethed, but they stayed silent. Al's own anger issues were another bone of contention for Claire. Since he grew up not just suppressing anger but often misdirecting it, Al had a tendency to displace his anger onto "safe" targets (in other words, someone like Claire, whom he loved and trusted) rather than direct it toward overbearing people whom he perceived as threatening (people who were, not coincidentally, the real hooks for his anger).

The issue became more volatile recently when Harriet was widowed and began making more demands on all of her adult children. Al's regular visits to his mother's home seemed to be prompted by a mix of realistic concern and unrealistic guilt. Claire was torn. "On the one hand, I understood his mother was getting older and needed extra attention," she says. "And I don't think Harriet is a deliberately cruel person. But on the other hand, when she continued to treat my husband as if he was a ten-year-old—and Al

reacted like a child who's fearful of being repri-
manded—well, I thought that was ridiculous!"

Things came to a head one day when Al and Claire
were having dinner at Harriet's house. "We were there
with Al's brother and his wife, laughing it up and having a great time," Claire recalled. "Harriet snapped at
all of us, saying it was rude to talk at the table. She actually cut me off in midsentence when I was trying to tell
a story, and told me 'OK, that's enough,' as if she were
correcting a five-year-old." Claire's fury at Harriet's
reprimand was only heightened when she saw Al's reaction: he got panicky and tried to correct Claire, not his
mother. "That was an extra slap in the face."

Clearly, this family had deep-seated issues surrounding the matter of respect. When Claire discussed the issue with me in a therapy session, we
talked about the various anger hooks that both she and
Al were encountering where Harriet was concerned.
Claire admitted she got hooked by Al's excessive attention to his mother. Since his attention to Harriet often
came at the expense of time with Claire, in a very real
sense Harriet was encroaching on Claire's territory.
Seeing Al behave so passively was another big hook,
made more obvious whenever Al snapped at Claire
while simultaneously knuckling under to Harriet. And
then, of course, there was the matter of Harriet's stern
reprimands to Claire herself. Lots of disrespect there!

Yet with each of these hooks, Claire came to see
an unmet need to be treated with more consideration.

Accordingly, she set out to address her need rather than continuing to bite the hook.

First, Claire spoke to Al about the practical matter of how frequently the couple visited his mother. "It had reached the point where we almost never had a free Saturday," she said. Claire believed they had to set limits so they could enjoy some leisure time alone together. And since Claire was able to initiate the discussion in a calm and non-accusatory way, Al didn't respond with his typical defensiveness. In fact, he told Claire how much he appreciated her willingness to tolerate his mother's rudeness; he admitted he was also frustrated by the frequency of their visits. Together, the pair set a commitment that—unless Harriet had a real medical or a major personal problem—they would see her no more than once a month.

From there, the couple was able to take a deeper look at the relationship patterns that impacted them all: mother, son, and daughter-in-law. Instead of accusing Al of being too passive (which would undoubtedly have made him feel disrespected and defensive), Claire offered understanding. She recognized how difficult it was to have a parent who was so demanding and critical. But Claire also made her own emphatic position statement. "I told Al our primary loyalty is to each other—our relationship comes first," she said. "While I'm willing to overlook some of Harriet's behavior, I'm not willing to honor her wishes at the expense of our relationship." Al, for his part, recognized that he would be wise to shed his peace-at-any-price demeanor and become more assertive with his mother.

Claire also suggested that Al had been suppressing his anger toward his mother and unfairly displacing it onto her. At first, Al didn't agree, and bristled at the very suggestion. But Claire gently persevered: she spoke of several occasions when Al had given up his Saturdays to run errands for his mother. On those occasions, nothing seemed to make Al happy. Claire calmly recounted these incidents, trying not to make her confrontation another hook for Al. Then she gave Al some time to mull things over (a mark of respect).

After some thought, Al agreed Claire might be right: he had been angry at his mother for all the demands on his free time. And since he found it hard to confront Harriet, Claire was often a safer target for his anger. He did some reflecting: "Is my mother ever really satisfied? It seems the more I jump to please her, the higher she keeps raising the bar." Perhaps this was self-defeating behavior, Al realized—especially if it had negative consequences on his marriage.

First and foremost, Claire and Al gained a new respect for each other's positions. And with that new-found resolve, they were able to handle the "Harriet issue" with more unity and even some humor. When Al told his mother he could only visit once a month, Harriet accused him of being neglectful; she pulled out her arsenal of guilt-instilling tactics—including that old gambit, "Your father would be so disappointed in you if he were here." And at times, Al battled the tendency to give in to whatever his mother wanted.

This is to be expected: even when we're devoted to making a change, it's difficult to alter our role in a particular relationship without returning to the same old patterns—especially when we're dealing with a parent who is intent on making our behavior conform to his or her agenda. Most of us have a strong desire to please our parents. Al had to keep telling himself that Harriet's harangues were a potent hook for him, and he refused to bite. Once, when Harriet branded Al "selfish" for not coming over to fix a leaky faucet, he calmly replied, "You know, Mom, you may be right. What I need to do is balance the time I can spend with you with the time I give my wife, my home, and my own work. It's not that I don't love you, but my resources are limited, and there are other aspects of my life that also need attention." Notice that Al's statement did not show any disrespect for his mother. But he did take a self-respecting stand for himself.

Ironically, Harriet gradually backed down when she realized her bombastic outbursts weren't having the desired effect. "She seems to be more pleasant whenever we see her, and more grateful for the things we do for her. Can you beat that?" Claire laughed. It seems that when Al and Claire set appropriate boundaries—and Harriet came to realize her guilt-inducing tactics weren't going to work—there was more respect all around.

What Not to Do When You're Angry: Compound the Disrespect

Learning to spot and address the need for respect is a new skill that takes some time. In fact, there is a steep learning curve at the beginning of this process. It is likely you will bite into a given hook a number of times before you are actually able to spot and avoid it. Too often, when that happens, it's easy to escalate not only the conflict, but the disrespect.

When we are angry, it is hard to fight fair. In a nutshell, fair fighting entails keeping the focus on the issue, not the other person's shortcomings; not making angry generalizations like "You always . . . "; not bringing up old grudges; not engaging in name-calling; and not making accusations against the other party. In a fair fight, each person takes responsibility for his own actions, and it is clear what each person feels and wants. But if you have just bitten an anger hook—or even if you're trying not to bite—it is a challenge to stay in fair-fight mode.

One couple, Jill and Peter, had a blowup over the matter of selling their house. When their daughter Jenna reached school age, the pair wanted to trade up and move to a town with a top-notch school district. So they put their current home on the market and received a few bids from prospective buyers. After receiving one solid offer, Jill and Peter discussed it quite seriously. Their real estate agent assured them the price was in line with market value. So, believing they had come to an agreement, Jill called the agent to accept the offer. But when she told Peter of her actions, he was furious: "How could you do such a thing? Don't you remember I said I wanted to sleep on it? You're so stupid, and now you've probably cost us money!"

Jill countered with a few accusations of her own: "You liar! Last night, you thought it was a good offer. Now you're changing your tune—*what else is new?* If I hadn't acted quickly, they probably would have backed out. It would be just like the time with that stock tip, when you hemmed and hawed and then it was too late!" Back and forth they went, each bitter accusation met with an equally harsh counterattack.

Things reached a crescendo when Jill told Peter to get out and stay with his brother. When he balked, she threatened to leave herself—and take their daughter with her.

This is a good example of "unfair" fighting. Both Jill and Peter felt disrespected because each had verbally abused the other. Both invoked extraneous issues, rehashing old business to prove their point. Both heaped insult upon injury, rejection upon humiliation. Yet neither one recognized the part they played in escalating the conflict. At first, neither Peter nor Jill was able to spot the unmet need for respect that triggered their anger.

But happily, this was one couple who did manage to turn things around. A few days later, when things had cooled, Jill apologized to Peter for the nasty things

she said, especially for calling him a liar. Her concilia-
tory gesture prompted Peter to be just as contrite: he
not only expressed regret for the cruel things he had
said but confided some of the issues that really upset
him. Peter said that when they put the house on the
market, he felt as if he was losing a big part of his identity. "It was a kind of jewel, something I had put a great
deal of work into . . . and now it was being taken away."

He also shared some insecurities about Jill's level of
commitment to him. Peter worried that she might see the
sale of their home as the wrong kind of "fresh start," an
opportunity to rethink whether she wanted to stay in the
marriage. But Jill made it clear that she loved Peter and—
despite a few marital sore points—was committed to
building a future with him: "Our security is wherever we
are together; it has nothing to do with a set of four walls."

Clearly, this couple had issues surrounding the sale
of their house that had very little to do with its selling price. When Peter and Jill both felt disrespected,
their anger became more intense and they became
polarized. But when they dealt with the underlying
issues that troubled them both, they were able to
become unhooked from that pointless rage—and
achieve a deeper understanding of what steps had to
be taken to meet both their needs.

A Question of Territory

Territory—turf—is the second unrecognized need
most often involved in triggering anger. We all have a

certain sense of our personal space, both physical and psychological. Generally, we are only dimly aware of this territorial need until someone violates a boundary. Suppose you routinely ride the train to work; this is your time to read the newspaper and catch up on current events to face the workday. On one morning, you make the commute sitting next to two people who are engaged in a long, loud conversation. Their talking and laughter is impossible to tune out, and you find it difficult to concentrate on your reading material. The train is crowded, so there is no possibility of changing seats.

Chances are you will feel a growing annoyance, the discomfiting sense that someone else's behavior is encroaching on your rights. Of course, the argument could be made that a train is public space—and conversation does *not* violate any legal statutes. But your anger, in this case, stems from a breach of personal space that has nothing to do with legalities. Your needs for routine, mental focus, and private time have all been upended. So—whether it's logical or not—you're angry!

The concept of territory speaks to a basic human need. In every society, there are laws to protect property and personal artifacts. In many parts of the United States, it's even legal to use certain types of violence in order to defend your land and personal possessions.

Social psychologists have long observed that humans have a way of establishing their own innate

Violating Our Boundaries, Trampling on Our Turf: Angry Situations Prompted by Breach of Territory

Whenever someone crosses the line—infringing on our physical or psychological space—we are apt to perceive the transgression as an anger hook.

Infringements on Physical Space
- Trespassing
- Stealing
- Borrowing something without returning it, or borrowing without permission
- Damaging property or treating it carelessly
- Getting too close to you
- Strong or offensive odors
- Loud noise or music

Infringements on Psychological Space
- Menacing glances
- Too many demands on your time
- Wanting too much intimacy
- Interruptions to your communication or train of thought
- Trying to control your choices

comfort zone, often compensating for too much closeness (a violation of territory) by adopting tactics that will preserve personal privacy. For instance, people living in big cities are sometimes labeled "aloof" because they tend to avoid eye contact and ignore strangers on the street. But this kind of behavior can serve an important adaptive function. It enables city dwellers to maintain a comfortable level of psychological distance even when they are living in physically crowded environments. In a very real sense, humans have found an ingenious way to automatically fill that basic territorial need.

And it is also true that territory is easily compromised in our complex, fast-paced, overcrowded world. Road rage is disturbingly commonplace; strangers get into altercations in long lines. How do you feel if someone cuts in a long line ahead of you? When a telemarketer calls in the evening—interrupting dinner, or waking the baby from a sound sleep—it can cause us to abruptly hang up or let loose with a barrage of angry words. Again, our private time, our territory, has been violated. Movie theaters, restaurants, and other public places post notices asking patrons to turn off cell phones, since this technological marvel of modern life—a vital convenience at the right time—can be an invasive nuisance to everyone's sense of personal space.

In some circumstances, even a wayward glance can be interpreted as a breach of territory. Men in our culture have a particular sensitivity around this issue; quite possibly, it's a holdover from the days when males felt a keen pressure to protect and defend the family from harm. I've seen young men exclaim "Who are *you* looking at?!" if they feel that someone is staring too intently at them or their girlfriends.

Indeed, intrusiveness of any kind is such a powerful force that another street term has cropped up to describe its effect on our psyches: *in your face*. If someone gets too close to you or your property, they're *in your face*—invading your turf—and it's likely to make you angry.

Identifying Boundary Violations

In families, opportunities for territorial clashes arise almost daily. Members of a family share living space, delegate household responsibilities, grapple with a host of time commitments, manage a budget, put up with one another's personality quirks, and interact in a hundred other ways that put boundary issues to the test. No wonder there are myriad ways anger can be triggered over breach-of-territory matters.

Lee, a twenty-four-year-old graduate school student, had mixed feelings about still living in her parents' home. "I'm stretched to the max as it is," she said. With school loans and a very demanding schedule— which included two part-time jobs along with a full academic courseload—it seemed like a practical solution for Lee to move back in with her parents until she finished her education. But after four years away at college, she was used to having more freedom.

Her parents, Bill and Helen, were also set in their ways. "We're only too happy to have Lee live at home," her mother said. "This way, she can concentrate on her studies without worrying about how she'll pay the rent and everything else. But sometimes it feels as if we're all over each other. Lee's schedule is different from ours; she stays out late on weekends and then sleeps in the next day. So we have to tiptoe around, not wanting to wake her up. Plus, she doesn't have the same mealtimes or even eat the same kinds of food that we do. The refrigerator is always stocked, but half the stuff is cordoned off as hers and the other half is ours. We've had some really petty fights when one of us mistakenly eats the other's food!"

The family room is another battleground. Lee sometimes wants to invite friends over to chill out and watch a movie, a reasonable enough request. But on weeknights, Helen and Bill prefer to stake their claim to this room: "It's our house, after all. And at the end of a long day, we just want a chance to relax and unwind." Conflicts over time, conflicts over space . . . it's the stuff family skirmishes are made of.

But a more enduring problem concerned Bill's habit of playing music at home and his daughter's objection to the constant onslaught of audio stimulation. "He has it blaring in the living room almost anytime he's home. If I'm trying to study—or if I just want a little quiet—I constantly have to keep asking him to turn it down. My dad doesn't seem to understand that sometimes the rest of us want a little peace and quiet." Helen is inclined to agree with Lee, so this particular dispute has become a gender rather than generational standoff.

Bill's side: "Music is my hobby, and listening to it helps me relax. They can both close the door if it bothers them. I don't complain when they're the ones with the TV blaring!" It sounds like a minor matter, but the music issue has created a chronic low-level hostility that pervades this household.

"It's like a constant imposition, something that feels inescapable," Lee says. In truth, it's a matter of territory—both mother and daughter are bristling because they feel they're being unwillingly subjected to unwanted sound. But Bill also has a legitimate desire: he would like to enjoy music in the privacy of his own home.

So who wins this particular turf battle? Whose needs should take precedence? Of course, the best solution is to try to negotiate a peaceful settlement in which everyone's boundaries are considered.

This family cleverly solved the problem when Helen came home one evening with a pair of noise-canceling headphones for Bill's iPod. Bill loved the wonderful sense of "feeling closer" to his music without the distracting sounds of household and street noises. And Lee wore the noise-canceling headphones without music playing when she needed to study and her dad was listening to his music on the stereo. Although she could hear his music, it sounded off in the distance and didn't interfere with her concentration. This solution allowed everyone to lay claim to his or her own territory, rather than engage in an endless round of turf skirmishes.

Other Territorial Disputes: Independence Versus Intimacy

Of course, some territorial lines are easy to spot: if one person savors quiet and another enjoys music, if one likes the window open and another wants it closed—you may not know the solution, but at least you now clearly know what the dispute is about. But not all matters of turf or territory are quite so apparent.

Sharon is the second child in her family, the younger of two daughters. For her entire life, she has had an unusual (if not always welcome) closeness with both her mother, Barbara, and her older sister, Terry. "I don't know what I would do without my daughters," says Barbara. "The three of us are best friends. There's nothing we can't tell each other."

Terry, who rarely challenges Barbara's view of anything, seems perfectly content with having an enmeshed mother-daughter relationship. She routinely calls Barbara several times a day, pops into her home unannounced, and seeks her advice on everything from recipes to her love life. For most of their childhood, she and Sharon had shared a similarly tight bond.

But as a young adult living on her own, Sharon began to feel stifled by so much closeness. "I'm really grateful to my mother and my sister; they've been very supportive of me my whole life," she says uneasily. "But where does it stop? They expect to know everything about my life—and frankly, some of it is none of their business." With a bittersweet laugh, Sharon tells a story of getting a call one day at work from her sister. "Terry was on her cell phone and said, 'Hey, I'm in your closet—could you tell me where you put your blue sweater?' OK, I did give her a key to my apartment—and we always raided each other's closets as kids—but *really!*"

A more hurtful incident concerned Sharon's recent relationship with a boyfriend, Curt. At first, Barbara and Terry wanted to know every detail of the budding romance. Yet when the two decided they weren't too crazy about Curt, Sharon became increasingly angry and defensive. She felt that her mother and sister had no business meddling, and frankly told them so.

Barbara was aghast: "How can Sharon talk to us that way? We're only trying to help! To think that she's putting a guy before *us*, her own family!" To Barbara, it seemed unthinkable that Sharon would want to navigate a love relationship without some good advice; she actually believed she, Terry, and Sharon all got an equal vote on the matter. Anger erupted and soon Sharon wasn't speaking to either her mother or her sister. Although she wanted to assert her independence, she felt bereft and sad about the estrangement from people she cared about.

Long after she and Curt broke up, Sharon continued to feel wary and conflicted. How close is too close? What are healthy boundaries to set in relationships with parents and siblings? Feeling a desire for closeness on the one hand and a wish for autonomy on the other can be a difficult territorial conundrum for any family member to face. In this case, it's not simply a matter of recognizing your need—it's realizing that the needs of you and the other person may be in conflict. When that happens, the key to reclaiming territory is to find your own boundaries.

How to Identify Your Own Needs for Respect and Territory

Once again, few of us consciously realize that interference with respect, territory, or both is a major cause of our anger—and once you can grasp this concept, it helps clarify precisely what needs must be fulfilled. If you discover that you are hooked and you are tempted to rant and curse, replace any standard four-letter expletive with a new one: *need*. Here are some questions to ask yourself to better home in on your need:

- In what way do I feel violated right now? Is it a lack of respect or a violation of territory that is making me angry?
- How would I change the situation if I could?
- Have I encountered this particular hook before? At what time, with what person or persons, and under what conditions?
- If this feels like a familiar hook, what happened when I encountered it in the past? Did I bite the hook? Did I get really angry? Did any damaging or enduring consequences occur?
- What is my need, right now in the moment? What would have to happen to make me feel that my needs for respect or territory are once again intact?
- What is my goal—not just for the moment, but in future interactions with this person or future occurrences of this situation?

The idea is to ask yourself the question before you get hooked, or as soon as possible thereafter. Say *hook*, then say *need*—and you will be well on your way!

Now that you understand Step Two—pinpointing the unmet needs for respect and territory that form the "core" of most anger hooks—it's time to proceed to the third and final step of anger management: how do you go about filling these needs?

Step Three:
Fill the Need

Now that you have become familiar with what hooks your anger—and with the fact that when a hook appears, it generally means a need fulfillment is being threatened—it's time to learn more about Step Three of anger management.

Once again, take out your Hook Book. If you have been keeping a record of anger hooks, take a few moments to review your recent entries. Or turn to a clean page, think back over the past week or so, and jot down two or three of the most memorable anger events that come to mind. Set things up much the way you did in the last chapter's exercise, making note of what need (respect or territory) was violated in each particular incident. Now it's time to add a third component—filling the need. So your Hook Book will have four columns: Anger Event, Hook, Need (this could be a biological need or a need for respect and territory), and last, Desire (what do I desire to get this need met?).

Let's revisit the example cited in the last chapter, in which you find yourself unwillingly pressed into service by a hostile department manager who wants some last-minute work on a project that's not your own. The set-up might look something like this:

Anger Event	Hook	Need	Desire
Manager demands last-minute Power-Point presentation without any notice	Injustice	Respect	Ample advance notice
Same manager insists you work on projects over the weekend	Injustice	Territory (your personal time)	To work during business hours

Or suppose you were to write about the annoyance of the frenzied dinner hour:

Anger Event	Hook	Need	Desire
Children kept interrupting me to help with homework when I'm cooking	Incompetence	Territory	Time to cook without distractions

Anger Event	Hook	Need	Desire
Children wouldn't stop; went on insisting even when I said I would help after dinner	Injustice	Respect	To set boundaries about when I am available to meet my family's needs

Here is how a few of the other anecdotes cited in the previous chapter might look if described in this Hook Book format. First, the story of Claire, Al, and Harriet (wife, husband, and mother-in-law) told from Claire's perspective; next, the travails of Barbara, Sharon, and Terry (a mother and two daughters), as conveyed by Sharon:

Anger Event	Hook	Need	Desire
Harriet "talks down" to us like children, tells us what to do, uses guilt to manipulate her son whenever she doesn't get her way	Injustice	Respect	To be treated like a mature adult
Expects us to visit more often than we would like	Injustice	Territory (time)	Visit less often

Anger Event	*Hook*	*Need*	*Desire*
Mom and Terry interfere with privacy decisions that are rightfully mine; they are too intrusive	Injustice	Respect	Autonomy

If these entries strike you as a bit too simplistic, don't worry: that is precisely the point. Part of what you are trying to do here is cut to the chase—that is, cull your complex anger issues down to their most rudimentary elements. When we are angry, many of us have a tendency to rehash every insult or replay an incident that proves how justified we are in feeling our rage. Instead of homing in on our own needs for respect and territory— and recognizing that these are central to our anger—we often go in circles, never reaching a resolution.

The Hook Book exercise is designed to bring such ruminations to a halt. In their place, you want to give yourself a clear-cut picture of not only what makes you angry, but also which unmet need may have to be addressed.

At this point, you may be wondering if your Hook Book will become a permanent bit of apparatus. The answer is no; it's a temporary tool to help you get acclimated to this new way of managing anger. In short order, the task of spotting hooks, recognizing needs, and figuring out how to address those needs will become, if not always easy, then at least more automatic.

How Is a Need Different from a Desire?

A *need* can be defined as anything that is necessary for life and well-being. Air, water, food, clothing, shelter, rest, and sleep . . . these are the basic survival needs. Our psychological needs include requirements for safety and stability, love and belonging, esteem and self-actualization. This second category also includes the needs for respect and personal territory.

Anger is likely to occur when a need is frustrated. This important point was first noted by two eminent psychologists, Neal E. Miller and John Dollard, in their now-famous "frustration-aggression" hypothesis, first published in 1939.

Needs are more basic and essential than wants or desires, which are preferences. For instance, we *need* food, but the choice of whether it's fish, meat, or vegetables is a *want* or *desire*. Similarly, we may need transportation, but whether to take a bus, train, or car is a *want*.

A central principle of this book is that people are often angered because their needs for respect and territory are threatened or not met. Recognizing and filling those needs is a key part of anger management. The point here: need fulfillment is *necessary* for well-being. Competing wants and desires are, however, much more

negotiable. For instance, if we are both hungry
(a need), but you want Italian food and I prefer
Chinese, we must find a compromise: perhaps the
local seafood restaurant. If we don't fill our need
for food, of course, we will both be unhappy.

Review Each Event

Once you have committed two or three anger events
to paper, step back and take a moment to study them.
Recall each incident. Try to view your list with a
detached, critical eye.

The first Hook Book assignment, described in
Chapter 5, offered instructions on how to spot your
anger hooks and how to describe the feelings that typically accompany them. In Chapter 6, you were shown
how to pinpoint the needs that are typically frustrated
by these anger-provoking events. Now you will focus
on the third and final step: how to substitute a need-
fulfillment response for each angry reaction.

Let's go back to the third anger event cited above—
children clamoring for your attention as you are busily
trying to make dinner. Take a moment to mentally
walk through the experience. What are likely to be
your anger hooks?

It's the end of a busy day. Your energy may be flag-
ging. Perhaps you are preoccupied with some lingering problems that cropped up earlier, such as a conflict

with a coworker or news that your latest cholesterol test is worrisome. As you walk into the kitchen, you notice the children's toys and homework scattered all around, and you set out to clear some counter space for dinner preparation. The phone rings. It's your mother-in-law wanting to recount her difficulties dealing with a plumber. Your ten-year-old comes in and asks how to spell *rhinoceros*. When you don't answer right away, he yells, "How am I supposed to finish my homework? You always help my sister, and you never help me!" While scurrying across the room to put the phone down, you accidentally kick the dog's bowl, spilling water that now has to be mopped up.

By now, you might be thinking, *If one more person makes one more demand on me, I'm going to explode!* Worse yet, you might be screaming, "Get out of here, leave me alone! It's *your* homework—I finished school a long time ago!" Even the poor hapless dog could be in for a kick: *If we hadn't gotten that puppy for the kids, the stupid bowl wouldn't have been there in the first place!*

So you have these anger hooks dropping down in quick succession: troubling things on your mind, a mess wherever you look, family members clamoring for your attention, an unexpected mishap. You could readily lose your cool or you could suddenly realize: *hook!* (Say it out loud if you like, to help define the situation precisely.)

And once you hear yourself say *hook*, the very next word you must utter is *need*. Immediately ask yourself, *What is my need?* At this particular moment in the middle of dinner preparations, you might conclude, *I need my territory, my personal space.* In short, you need a moment to regroup and collect yourself.

Now fill that need. In this scenario, filling the need might go something like this: You gently but firmly tell your ten-year-old you will help him shortly. Instruct him to please go to his room and you will be there very soon, and then sit down. Take a couple of deep breaths. Collect yourself so you can prioritize the issues confronting you (the ability to tackle these tasks on *your terms* is a way of reclaiming territory). You may decide to mop up the water first, then go to your son with dictionary in hand, showing him how to look up not only this word but future unknown words himself. Then you may wish to return to the kitchen and calmly focus on getting dinner ready. And should the phone ring again while you're cooking, you decide to let the answering machine pick up.

Surprisingly, it may only take a few moments to collect yourself in such circumstances. If you are able to resist biting the hook and can focus instead on filling the need, you might be pleasantly surprised to see how effectively you can thwart your usual angry reaction. Whenever you hear yourself say *hook*, follow it with *need*. That is your signal to craft a need-fulfillment response.

How to Deal Directly with the Need

This dinnertime frenzy is an example of how anger hooks can be predictable—you have a good idea of when and where they're going to drop down. And that enables you to look ahead and try to fulfill those needs for respect and territory in advance. *In advance* is the operative phrase here, since anticipating hooks—and devising ways to avoid biting them—is a key part of anger management.

Picture this: it's the start of another harried evening. Instead of rushing headlong into the tasks at hand, plan to first take two or three minutes for yourself. Perhaps do a few yoga stretches, read a magazine article, or do anything else that helps you unwind. Or perhaps what you most desire is to take ten minutes—uninterrupted—to do some straightening up, to unclutter your space so you can effectively work in it.

As for the barrage of homework demands: you might sit down with the children to set new ground rules or boundaries. Call a family meeting at a time when things are low-key and everyone is relaxed. Initiate a respectful dialogue: "I know that things tend to get a little frenzied in the evenings, and I sometimes lose my temper. The truth is, I don't mean to say hurtful things to you—and I really do want to be available to help with your homework. But I want some things from you, too. For starters, I would like to be able to focus on one thing at a time, especially when I'm trying to make dinner."

From there, you might consider some practical alternatives that accommodate everyone's wishes—designate a set time for homework, either before or after the dinner hour; get the children to hit the books in their own rooms, rather than further cluttering the kitchen table; let them know what time you will be available to address academic queries. In short, keep your eyes on the prize: the need-fulfillment response.

Suppose you recall an incident when you were annoyed because your daughter borrowed an article of clothing without asking—a breach of both respect (for not asking) and territory (it's your scarf). Rather than respond angrily, for example, "What gives you the right to help yourself to my clothes? You are so inconsiderate," address the needs that were violated and how they might be better met in the future: "Please return my scarf. I'm happy to lend you my clothes, but last time you didn't return what you borrowed. I was annoyed that you just took my scarf without asking." Such a statement clearly lets your daughter know how her actions affected you; it doesn't disparage her or accuse her of selfishness. But it does firmly insist that in the future, you need to be respected and your property (your territory) has to be honored.

Or imagine that your son's surly backtalk hooks you into an argument; within minutes, the two of you are shouting at one another. As you hear yourself saying, "If I mouthed off to my father like that, I'd be smacked into the middle of next week!" stop and say *hook*. Spot your own need to regain respect. Then think of what response might fill that need. You might shift gears with your son and say, "It makes me uncomfortable when we talk this way."

Notice that this phrase is not an inflammatory accusation; it is a non-judgmental observation. "We are talking in a way that makes me uncomfortable. Let's change the tone so we can understand each other and stop fighting. At the same time, let's try to get to the root of the problem. What's bothering you?" Then listen to his concerns. Don't try to dispute them. Hear how *he* perceives the situation. You can ask, "Do you mean . . . ?" and at least come to an agreement about what you are disagreeing about before trying to resolve the conflict. (This technique is called mirroring and will be discussed further later on.)

Maybe you also find yourself grappling with anger-provoking events from the other side of the generational divide: your mother expects you to contact her every day (a breach of territory) and lays on the guilt trip and sarcasm (a lack of respect) if the phone doesn't ring right on schedule. The "old you" would have seethed silently or bristled outwardly at such disrespectful treatment—first, because your mother doesn't understand that your personal demands might make it difficult to call so frequently; and second, because Mom never thinks *she* should be the one to initiate the contact.

But the "new you"—who has learned to spot the hook and insert a need-fulfillment response—sees a different approach to the dilemma: "Mom, my life is so busy that sometimes I can't predict when I'll be able to call (territory). And I tend to get a little defensive when you take this personally and call me selfish (respect). Then we start fighting, and we both lose. So maybe we could try a new system: I'll call you when I can, and you call me if you would like to talk."

Notice that this approach gets to the heart of the matter by focusing directly on the needs for territory and for respect. Instead of getting sidetracked with extraneous issues (for example, all the other times your mother made unreasonable demands or which of you is the more selfish), you clearly outline your needs and how they might be met through a more fair and flexible way of staying in touch.

A word of caution: when first starting to practice anger management, people often remember what they were "supposed to do" after the fact—that is, after they have already reacted to the hook in a characteristically angry way. (Even seasoned anger management "experts" still fail on occasion. I certainly do!) Realize that occasional backslides are inevitable. Don't be discouraged if you sometimes find yourself handling a situation in the old way, by letting Mom have it or yelling "Because I said so!" to your son.

Realize, instead, that managing anger is hard work. You are trying to adopt a new way of responding and retooling the habits of a lifetime. When my patients get disheartened, I remind them that I've seen many people face a similar kind of disappointment in themselves when they revert to old behavior patterns. But with repeated efforts, those same people have greatly improved their anger management skills. Believe in yourself; keep trying and you *will* make progress. Respect yourself for making the effort—even if it sometimes fails.

Selfishness Versus Healthy Self-Interest

Am I suggesting that you should reduce your anger by becoming preoccupied with your own needs, by turning self-centered and inconsiderate? Absolutely not! But how do you focus on your own wishes without appearing to be selfish?

First, it's important to emphasize that there is nothing wrong or selfish about having needs, wants, and wishes—and seeking healthy ways to get them met. Quite the contrary: it's a hallmark of maturity to be able to actualize your needs and desires. It only becomes selfish if you take the stance that your wishes always come first, without considering that those around you are equally worthy and just as entitled to their needs and wants. Being attuned to someone else's needs is an admirable quality; often, that generosity of spirit is just the catalyst to help defuse anger and promote understanding. But how far can you go to meet another's needs and desires? Is there a point when you do more harm than good by giving too much?

I often share a situation from my own life as an example of anger reduction through need fulfillment. Years ago, I was a psychology doctoral student at New York University, living in a Greenwich Village apartment, and a passionate student of the piano. My practice sounds were sufficiently musical that a neighbor introduced me to a legendary jazz pianist, Paul Bley. Paul said that if I truly wanted to learn how to play jazz, it was necessary to learn in "real time," by performing onstage with those who are skilled at improvising. He even gave me a chance: "Meet me in Europe next month and bring your electric keyboard. It's unlikely there will be two keyboards at the gig. You'll have a chance to play with some excellent musicians."

A month later, grappling with a suitcase in one hand and a heavy electric organ in the other, I boarded a plane for Amsterdam. Eventually, I arrived at the site of a very respectable festival in Toulon, France, where many noted American jazz stars were set to perform in a lovely outdoor amphitheater. There was time for just one rehearsal with the band Paul had hired. And I was terrible! Since I was not all that familiar with Paul's music—which has little structure and much nuance—my keyboard playing was overstated, like a lumbering elephant walking on fine silk cloth. After the rehearsal, Paul said, "Robert, we have to talk. . . . "

I felt awful. I had excitedly traveled across the Atlantic, lugging a sixty-pound keyboard, and I had blown it. But Paul, who was as subtle and soft-spoken as his music, said, "I believe you can help someone only as much as you can afford to. After that, it isn't really constructive. How about playing one tune in the concert?"

It felt like a huge weight had been lifted off my shoulders. I would not have to return to the United States feeling like a failure—yet I also did not have to worry about ruining the concert. I felt fairly confident that I could learn one song for the next day.

The big night arrived—and it was cold! Paul's performance started out well, but as the evening wore on, the temperature had a chilling effect on everyone's technique; the musicians could barely move their fingers. I was scheduled to play the very last piece. The song was loud and fast (sure-fire crowd pleasers) and I was a new source of energy for both the audience and the musicians. More than twenty-five years later, I can still feel the excitement of the improvised musical dialogue and the applause of the crowd. It was thrilling.

Paul's words—"You can help someone only as much as you can afford to"—were a bull's-eye. If you don't take sufficient care of your *own* interests, no one will benefit. Had Paul been pressured into allowing me to play more than my skills warranted, he would have been angry that I ruined his concert. Had he not given me a chance to play at all, I would have been angry that he had "led me on" all the way to Europe (after all, he had heard me play in New York before issuing the invitation). Paul helped me as much as he could afford to—as much as was feasible to address both our interests—and we both won.

When it comes to need fulfillment, it's important to bring a bit of healthy self-interest to the table. This is very different from selfishness; when a person acts selfishly, he asserts that only *his* needs matter. Think of it this way: if you don't take care of yourself, it's unlikely anyone else will. And if you don't get some of your own desires met, it's unlikely you'll be well-poised to fulfill anyone else's. A well-known quote from the Talmud puts forth the challenge handily: "If I am not for myself, then who will be for me? But if I am for myself only, then what am I?" If you can be your own advocate while still being a champion for others, then everyone can benefit.

Another Helpful Tactic: The Mirroring Technique

One of the best ways to understand other people's issues is to imagine what it feels like to be in their shoes. Empathy is an identification with and understanding of another's situation, feelings, and motives. Clearly, it's a wonderful quality to cultivate when you are trying to manage anger effectively and compassionately.

Usually, though, when you're about to get hooked by an anger-provoking situation, empathy goes right out the window. Anger has a way of making us rigid, more convinced of the rightness of our own position. It's our adversary who should change! When two opponents are both coming from this position—each similarly convinced that he is "right"—communication tends to shut down. Not surprisingly, this is not conducive to an empathic mind-set.

I often recommend that my patients learn a technique called *mirroring*. When in conflict, consciously try to serve as a *mirror* for the other person's position; reflect back to them what you believe they are saying. This method offers two big advantages. First, it helps you better understand the other person's perspective. Second, when you mirror someone it helps that person feel understood and respected. This second advantage can be key in reaching a happy outcome and maintaining a positive relationship.

Here is an example: Your twelve-year-old son is giving you a hard time about starting his homework: despite repeated warnings, he's dawdling in front of the TV or mindlessly playing video games. Your first impulse is to yell, "Turn that set off and get those books open this minute!" From there, it is likely your child will come back with the "five more minutes" wheedle, a host of "good reasons" for his actions, or an angry challenge: "Why don't you get off my back? You're the biggest nag!"

But instead of engaging in this kind of mindless back-and-forth, take a moment to see the situation from your child's viewpoint. Maybe he needs some quiet time before launching into his studies. Perhaps his delaying tactics are masking some anxiety; he might be having difficulties mastering the fine points of algebra but be reluctant to ask for help. If you take a moment to examine these possibilities, it can give a new slant to things.

First, ask how he is doing. Then try to mirror what he may be feeling: "Do you mean that you feel drained from today's activities and were playing video games because you needed to relax a little before doing your homework?" Open the lines of communication; let your child know that his viewpoint matters. You may be pleasantly surprised at the reaction you get.

Children usually become responsible for their actions when they feel they are understood rather than hounded. In this scenario, it's likely your mirroring would encourage your son to open up and share his misgivings about his homework. He might feel relieved to know he can share his vulnerabilities (that is, worries about grasping a particularly difficult subject) without fear of punishment. If he knows he can negotiate with you—that you will respect his need for a few minutes of downtime, or get him some extra tutoring help—he won't have to be defensive about sharing his concerns.

Of course, this doesn't mean a parent should not provide guidance or set limits—or respectfully insist that homework get done. Parents have a responsibility to teach their children effective ways of functioning and healthy ways to get their needs and desires met. It's *how we do it* that is critical. Yelling and screaming at children may cow them into submission, but it doesn't teach them how to juggle life's various demands. Nor does it demonstrate ways to manage anger effectively. But mirroring your child's feelings can do both those things: in a very real sense, you are setting an example for your child about how to avoid unproductive anger while also encouraging him to thrive.

Imagine a different scenario: you are concerned that your elderly father—who has started to have some difficulties with his hearing and eyesight—is no longer capable of driving safely. Dad, however, is stubbornly insistent that everything is "just fine, and you have no right to tell me what to do!" Your worry escalates when he has a minor fender bender. Your father continues to tell you to butt out and mind your own business. It *is* your business, you think; you accuse Dad of being selfish and irresponsible—can't he see that he could seriously injure himself or an innocent bystander? He insists his driving skills are fine. Result: the two of you aren't speaking, and nothing is resolved.

Now imagine using the mirroring technique to approach your father. Instead of confronting Dad with your concern, try to imagine the issues he's grappling with. He might be distressed by the unwelcome changes aging brings, his diminished capabilities and decreased stamina. *How will I cope?* he wonders. But instead of acknowledging those fears he might be hiding them with angry bravado.

First, ask him, "How are you feeling about that little accident?" Open a dialogue. If he says he doesn't want to talk about it, you can try mirroring anyway: "Dad, I'm concerned about you. I can see how you must be feeling, too: you've always taken pride in maintaining your independence. And now you're probably worried that that's going to change. Is that how you see it?" Notice how this approach is both respectful and sympathetic; it doesn't downplay the issue at hand, but it does offer an empathic understanding of the emotional turmoil your dad likely faces.

Mirroring helps get to the heart of the matter. It enables you to get beyond anger so you can focus more readily on the issues. In this case, you might say, "Dad, I understand your concerns. My goal is to keep you as independent as possible. But if you're having trouble driving, you realize how that could put you and others at risk; if you should be injured, that would be a bigger threat to your independence. So let's see how we can get you some help so you can manage things." This addresses both your father's need for territory as well as practical matters (the need, perhaps, for a twice-weekly car service to help Dad run his errands safely).

How to Deal with Someone Who Is in a Rage

Is it possible to practice smart anger management skills when you are dealing with someone in a rage? Granted, it's not easy. When a person is screaming accusations and expletives, it is difficult not to get hooked yourself, not to become defensive and respond in kind. What *is* helpful? Listen without interruption! An individual's anger, however seemingly irrational to you, always makes sense to him in the moment. Let the person finish his remarks. You can even ask if he has finished and if it's OK to respond now. Do your best to mirror what he is saying so he believes that you are at least trying to understand his point of view. This often helps to calm things down.

The least effective course of action is to challenge the enraged individual. This is like waving a red flag in front of a charging bull—it only makes the bull charge harder. If you find you cannot make any headway—if an angry person is totally unreceptive—the best course is to respectfully leave the scene. You might say, "It doesn't seem as if what I'm saying is coming across. If we continue, we might say things that will leave us both feeling hurt, and nothing will be resolved. So let's plan to revisit this at a time when we can get through to one another more effectively." This tactic may take some self-restraint, but it will give a difficult situation the best chance for resolution. As psychologist Silvan Tomkins has pointed out, "Anger is the emotion that makes a bad situation *worse.*"

Be Prepared to Revisit Your Needs Often

By now, you are probably becoming more adept at the anger management techniques outlined in the Hook Book: spot the hook, identify the need, fill the need. Through time and practice, this three-part process will become more and more automatic.

Review the issues surrounding your needs for respect and territory, because similar issues are likely to crop up again. The idea is to be prepared in advance with need-fulfillment responses to anger-provoking hooks. That will help you minimize your anger.

Joanna is a twenty-six-year-old art therapist living on her own in an apartment two towns away from her parents' home. Though she savors her freedom, Joanna often drops in on her mom and dad to enjoy a home-cooked meal or just to catch a movie on TV or discuss the high points of the evening news together.

But, like many young adults, Joanna often feels like she somehow falls into outmoded ways of relating to her parents—particularly when she is in their home, on their "turf." She sometimes feels they don't sufficiently respect her independence. And she spots the ways they can still hook each other over little things: "In many ways my parents still treat me as a child; they think I should still be 'obedient,'" Joanna says. But she is also learning how to put these anger management techniques into practice.

"The other night, as we were all watching TV, a commercial for a diet product came on, featuring a well-known actress who is now overweight," Joanna recalls. "My father said, 'How could she let herself get so out of shape? It's a shame because she's so attractive otherwise.' Well! Was *I* hooked! The weight comment was one thing, since I tend to be obsessive about my own eating habits. Then I resented the implication that a woman's worth is based on how she looks. Plus, how can my father assume that people just *let* themselves get out of shape? It's so much more complex than that!"

Joanna's first reaction was to snap at her father: "You know how worthless that makes me feel? You know I have eating issues, but you still make an insensitive comment like that. And besides, this person is working hard to lose weight—I think she deserves credit, not criticism." Joanna's mother chimed in to support her daughter's viewpoint. At that, Joanna's father got defensive, and the group—now aligned two-against-one by gender—were on the verge of exchanging angry barbs.

But then Joanna caught herself: *hook*. Joanna felt her father's comments were *unjust*; she wanted him to respect one of her important issues (her concerns about weight); at the same time, she felt he could show more understanding toward anyone who struggles with dieting difficulties, substance abuse, or similar problems. Joanna also recognized something else: she was hooking her father. "Since I'm studying psychology, my dad thinks I'm always analyzing him," she says with a laugh. "So whenever we disagree, he thinks his flaws are showing, that I'm putting him down—and he gets his back up! When my mother agreed with me, he must have felt we were really ganging up and disrespecting him."

Before the argument got out of hand, Joanna calmly switched tactics. "You know, Dad, maybe I read you wrong; you may have meant that remark in a sympathetic way. Sometimes I get a bit defensive about weight issues because I know I've struggled with a few of my own. And I admire anyone who takes steps to address them." Joanna's comment served to meet her father's need for respect: she gave him the benefit of the doubt and opened up a rational dialogue without firing back, lecturing him on addictive behavior, or sacrificing her own stance on the issue. This helped defuse the potential blowup and paved the way toward better communication.

Anger management may not be quite like what they say about riding a bicycle—"once you learn how, you never forget." In truth, you will continue to take a spill now and then as you navigate this new road. But with practice and confidence, you *will* learn to maintain the right balance and become more and more sure-footed as you go along.

Wait, There's More: Additional Keys to Anger Management

When people first begin making changes—implementing the basics of the three-step anger management plan—it often sparks a "Eureka!" reaction. Patients come back with great enthusiasm, eager to share stories of how they are suddenly able to spot and avoid their own anger hooks. Knowing what to do when those hooks drop down makes many situations appear quite different. Being able to perceive anger hooks reframes many life events. Just as a new frame can heighten the beauty of a painting, seeing an anger-provoking situation as a "hook" can change the way we perceive our lives and choices.

Another happy result: patients say the people around them are pleased at the change anger management brings and grateful to have a cooler, more

173

composed family member in their midst. "It makes a big difference!" seems to be the prevailing sentiment of spouses, children, and others in the household: "Lo and behold, she [or he] is getting better." Often, if the anger management practitioner starts to regress, the family will be the first to encourage her to "get with the program" once again.

Of course, family members—however enthusiastic—can still continue to toss out those anger hooks. And you may occasionally still continue to bite. Ideally, anger management is a group effort, an endeavor everyone undertakes together. But even if you are doing it solo—even if those hooks are still out there—you will probably find yourself biting less and less frequently.

Beginning an anger management program is a bit like starting an exercise routine. With each milestone—another few laps in the pool, an additional mile on the treadmill, an appealing hook avoided—you will feel more accomplished and confident. Inevitably, there will be setbacks, times when your stamina is not up to par or your resistance to being hooked is less than ideal. But your best approach is to accept occasional lapses, take a few deep breaths, and get back in the game. This chapter offers additional strategies to help you do just that.

Ignoring Old Hooks, Setting New Rules

Sometimes when you stop biting hooks and start filling needs, you have to make a few changes in your relationships. Setting new guidelines with loved ones is often an integral part of this strategy. Altering certain ground rules can be vital if you want to reclaim respect and territory.

Kim is a smart, attractive single woman in her early forties who has many friends and a thriving career in publishing. She regards her life as rich and happy—but her mother can't seem to get past the fact that Kim isn't married. "She constantly makes these belittling remarks, trying to make me feel terrible about myself," Kim says. "I try to laugh it off, but it really makes me angry."

On one occasion, after a family party, Kim's mother called and offered to buy her a new skirt "because the one you were wearing on Sunday was really unflattering—and maybe if you dressed up a little more, men would find you more attractive." Another pivotal incident occurred when Kim shared the news that her friend Paula was getting married: "My mother went on and on about how great Paula is, how she had her life so together, and so on," Kim says. "That was the last straw." Tempers flared. Kim and her mother exchanged a barrage of angry accusations ("Why do you *always* treat me like I'm some kind of loser?") and counter-accusations ("Here I'm just trying to help you, and *this* is the thanks I get!"). As is the case in so many angry interactions, the real issues were never addressed or resolved.

But when Kim came to see that her mother's attitude was a potent anger hook, she resisted the urge to bite. Instead, she focused on recognizing her own need (to be respected) and set out to get that need met. With a calm demeanor, Kim approached her mother to set down new ground rules: "Mom, this whole thing about whether or not I'm married has turned into a real hot-button issue between us. I'm an adult with a very happy life—maybe I'll get married some-day, maybe I won't. But being single doesn't make me inadequate."

From there, Kim suggested that, from her view-point, their relationship would be happier if certain subjects didn't come up. "I find it painful to talk about my marital status or anything related to my appear-ance—or to hear unflattering comparisons with my friends. So from here on out, I'm asking that we make a conscious effort to avoid those topics." Kim's mother was initially defensive, and she repeated what she believed was her intention, that she was "only trying to help"—but Kim held firm. "Mom, I'm sure that's your intent, but it doesn't come across as helpful to me. From my standpoint, things between us would be a lot better—and I'd enjoy your company a lot more—if I knew you'd respect my wishes on this mat-ter." Kim made her position clear and her mother eventually (if a bit reluctantly) agreed to the new guidelines.

For a few weeks, things between Kim and her mother seemed to be cordial, if not exactly warm and fuzzy. Then on Valentine's Day, a new problem erupted. "At the end of the day, my father called to tell me my mother was mad because I hadn't called or sent a card," Kim said. "To me, it was totally out of left field. I mean, *Valentine's Day?* I could see if it was Mother's Day, but I think of Valentine's Day as a couples' holiday."

Though she was annoyed by her mother's response (and her father's intrusion), Kim decided to swim around this particular hook and not take the bait. She called her mother the next day intending to have a cheery conversation, without dwelling on the Valentine's Day "massacre." But she barely had time to say hello before her mom laid into her. "You're so neglectful! You don't listen to my advice, and look where it's gotten you. If you treat people this badly, no wonder you're not married!"

Kim was stricken. Though it was hard not to bite the succession of anger hooks her mother was luring her with, she did manage (partly out of shock) to terminate the conversation and get off the phone quickly. But as the incident replayed in her head over and over again, Kim found herself getting angrier and angrier. Not only had her mother hooked her—hurling a succession of hurtful, abusive accusations her way—but she had ignored the new guidelines Kim had worked so hard to establish.

In the face of Kim's newfound assertiveness—her respectful declaration of what she would and wouldn't tolerate in their relationship—her mother seemed to be reverting to the more familiar way of interacting. She could not let go of her mind-set about wanting her daughter to be married and seemed to displace that wish as a complaint about the Valentine's card. In a sense, she found a way to make those hooks loom larger and appear more menacing, with nearly irresistible bait.

At first, Kim was angry. But she knew she had a choice—to respond, rather than react, to her mother's tastily baited hooks. For the moment, Kim decided to do nothing at all. She knew she needed to give herself time to regain a more objective stance.

Surprisingly, it was Kim's mother who made the next move. "She left a message on my answering machine that said 'Let's just put the last forty-eight hours behind us,'" Kim reports. "Part of me wanted to say, 'Oh sure, you want it just the way *you* want it!' But another part of me recognized that she was a bit scared, nervous that she really had overstepped her bounds. I had to give myself time to think about how I'd respond to the situation."

Again, Kim had to ask herself: *What is my need and how do I fill it?* With that in mind, she carefully crafted her response. "Within a day, I called her back and calmly let her know where I stood. I told her I appreciated her phone call, her attempt to reach out. At the same time, I said her actions wounded me deeply, so I needed some time to sort things through. I was afraid I'd be too reactive if I attempted to talk to her now; in the present moment, I was vulnerable to getting hooked again. I didn't cut off the relationship in any way, but I did make it clear that I needed a kind of time-out. Then I did give myself the time I needed before resuming any interaction with my mother."

To her surprise, Kim's mother accepted her daughter's polite-but-firm position statement. Kim had made it clear that she was not about to return to the old ways of interacting: she would not react to anger-provoking tactics in the same old ways. Instead, Kim and her mother would have to establish a new norm, a healthier new way of relating to one another in the future.

The Value of a Time-Out

Part of effective anger management is planning ahead of time how we will respond to inevitable ups-and-downs, to the hooks that drop in front of us. This kind of advance preparation allows us a quicker, more effective response—one with less anger and distress.

One valuable tool we can adopt is the time-out. The wisdom of a time-out was noted as far back as the sixteenth century by the French philosopher-essayist Montaigne when he stated, "Things truly seem different to us once we have quieted and cooled down." The sentiment was echoed by Thomas Jefferson in his famous admonition, "If angry count to ten, if very angry count to one hundred."

The now-common strategy of a time-out is often used in the school setting, and it is designed to give children positive lessons in managing anger. If a particular child is behaving in an angry fashion—yelling, losing control, or physically striking out at another— teachers often insist that the instigator take a time-out. The technique entails separating the child from whatever conditions triggered her anger; it also provides a cool-down period so she may regain composure and see the circumstances more clearly.

For both adults and children, a time-out can be quite helpful. For children, the tactic often involves moving the child to another room—a specified part of the classroom or a "time-out chair"; at home, the child's bedroom is the most likely site for a time-out. The idea is to take ten or fifteen minutes (and sometimes more) to move an excited child to quieter surroundings.

It is not meant to be punitive. Ideally, the adult in charge—whether parent or teacher—is firm but sympathetic; the youngster can engage in whatever quiet activity she chooses, such as reading a book or even playing a video game. Afterward, the events triggering the time-out are briefly discussed. The time-out typically ends with an apology for the offending behavior, and hopefully, some insight into avoiding another such incident.

Am I suggesting you reward your child for misbehaving? Absolutely not! However, you should be alert to the possibility that a child may try to act out and purposely instigate a time-out so she *can* play video games! Be smart: if you suspect that is the case, provide another quiet, though less rewarding, activity.

Be sure the child is not isolated in a frightening way during a time-out. A time-out respects the fact that a child may be momentarily agitated or impulsive rather than *deliberately* mean and hurtful. So the idea is to create a temporary "safe" place, a spot where anger can be processed and where the child can "cool down" without negative consequences.

For adults, a time-out has to be self-initiated, of course, but the principle is much the same: make a conscious effort to separate yourself from whatever is making you angry. Go to another room. Take a walk. If the anger-provoking issue is a looming and complex one, such as Kim's hurtful encounter with her mother, you may need a longer time-out. That is, you may have to give yourself some days or weeks—some greater psychic distance—to mull things over and decide your most effective response. In a metaphorical sense, you are trying to get the hook out of your mouth and let your emotional wounds heal.

There is something else to bear in mind whenever you initiate a time-out: you cannot revisit the source of your anger too quickly. Returning a child to the same environment that triggered his anger will likely result in a near-instantaneous resumption of that anger. In other words, if the bait is still there, the temptation to bite is likely to be there, too! It is necessary for a degree of detachment to occur. Detachment can help us—or help an angry child—to reframe the situation in order to see the circumstances differently.

A Few Words About Punishment

It's generally not wise for a parent to punish a child in the heat of anger. But that doesn't mean a parent should not *ever* punish a child. Wait until you have cooled down. When you're angry, it's often useful to say, "I'll figure out what your punishment is later, when I'm calmer." And then *do it*! If you don't follow through with an appropriate punishment as stated, children will learn that what you say doesn't matter. They will get the idea that their parents are ineffective. If they absorb that message over a lifetime from their parental role models, they may then be on their way to becoming ineffective parents themselves.

There are a few guidelines to remember about punishment: First, make sure your child knows what is expected of him or her—what behavior is allowed, and what misbehavior will result in a punishment. It can be confusing for a child to be disciplined for something he or she didn't know was wrong. Second, punish promptly once you've cooled down. If days or weeks go by, the punishment will lose its impact and effectiveness. Third, when you do punish, be sure to match the severity of the punishment to the seriousness of your child's misdeed.

The Fine Art of Detachment

Detachment is an important key to anger management. The dictionary definition is "the act or process of disconnecting or detaching; separation." On the face of it, that might not sound like a good thing—it might seem to convey the idea of aloofness, a refusal to acknowledge the importance of issues or look things "squarely in the face." (Actually, that's closer to another "d" word—*denial*—but we'll get to that shortly.)

Detachment is altogether different from denial. To understand the difference, think about the anger management techniques described so far: the ability to spot a hook, identify a need, and devise a way to get that need filled. Each of these requires some degree of separation (or detachment) from your initial impulse to go for the bait. It's necessary to train yourself to step back and become an observer of *you*, to look at what is going on objectively in much the same way an outsider would see the fish about to get ensnared. Clearly, this isn't easy! But it is a skill well worth cultivating. Detachment can go a long way toward helping you gain mastery over your angry reactions.

As with other anger management techniques, detachment is a skill that takes practice. You want to develop an "observing self," an inner monitor that is trained to say *hook* and *need* at the right moment. Remember those cartoons that give an illustrative picture of conscience—the personal struggle between good and evil—by showing an angel sitting on one shoulder and a devil on the other, each whispering into the person's ear? You can picture an observing self in a similar way: a mini-version of you sitting on your shoulder, viewing an anger-provoking scenario, and whispering: "Wait! Danger! Stop! Don't bite! Is there a hook beneath that 'good reason' to become angry? Let's see what this situation is really about." From that fictitious vantage point on your own shoulder, you are better able to see the whole picture; in other words, you are better positioned to spot and avoid the hook and identify the need.

Without the capacity to detach, we are forever at the mercy of our impulses, rather than our intelligence. We stay *reactive*. And if we simply react as we always have, there will be no improvement in our capacity to manage anger. Take Kim's situation: if she had reacted to her mother's guilt-inducing phone call by following her first impulse, chances are she would have become furious. Kim might have fired back with a host of justifiable counter-accusations.

But she was becoming adept in the art of detachment: she was able to stand back from her own fury. From there, Kim saw the bait (her mother's words), with the hook lurking just beneath; the unfilled need (for respect); and the way to get that need met (a time-out from her mother and setting clear limits about her hot-button issues). Kim knew if she tried to resume a normal relationship too quickly—before she had

ample time to process the situation and cool down—
she stood a high chance of having her anger reactivated yet again.

Like any acquired skill, detachment doesn't happen overnight, nor does it occur without a few setbacks and missteps (yes, there will still be times when
you will be too immersed in your angry reactions to
see things as a detached onlooker). But like any
acquired skill, detachment improves with practice.
And learning to observe your own behavior will help
you become both more insightful and less impulsive.

Denial: How Can You Know?

Earlier in this book, we looked at the phenomenon of
anger in disguise. People can literally be angry without even knowing it: such individuals often have a pattern of understanding themselves more through their
thoughts than their feelings. They can become adept
at using denial as a "blocking device" to hold anything
unpleasant at bay.

Instead of acknowledging their own anger, some
individuals become overly judgmental, taking aim at
anything or anyone who appears to challenge their
belief system. As Carol Tavris wrote in *Anger: The Misunderstood Emotion*, "As a general strategy of information processing, denial and self-delusion protect us
against anger, depression, and anxiety, which is why
they are such characteristic responses to information
that threatens our basic view of the world."

A cognitive style rooted in denial lends itself to moral posturing, hypercritical commentary, and disapproval of the world at large and family members in particular. The judgmentally angry person tends to hold a rigid view of what is right and wrong, and her conversation is sprinkled with many references to "shoulds": "Children *should* do as they're told!" "A good mother *should* stay home with her children." "It's wrong to get a divorce—you made your bed, now lie in it." A great deal of anger is embedded in "should" statements like these—yet if you mention to a judgmental person, "Gee, you seem angry," it is likely she will insist that you are wrong while bristling with indignation!

Passive-aggressive behavior is another form of anger in disguise. Missed appointments, agreeing to everything but failing to follow through on most promises, or two-faced compliments ("You would look so great if only you could do something with that hair. . . .") are typical ways that individuals manage to both deny their anger and simultaneously make it known to others.

Sometimes when people are first learning anger management techniques, it's easy to think that *don't bite the hook* means *don't admit you're angry*. Think about it: your boss berates you in front of coworkers, and you inwardly say *hook*. And you know the next word you should mentally say to yourself is *need*, but it isn't easy to get a need for respect filled by a screaming boss, especially when you feel you have to maintain your professional composure. So you tell yourself, *I'm not biting that hook! I'm not angry!*

Anger management does *not* mean anger denial. Rather, it means consciously choosing how to respond to the anger-provoking events, and making choices that are respectful to both yourself and others. By simply denying you are angry, you set up the possibility that anger will manifest in some other way: as some of the judgmental or passive-aggressive behavior just noted, or perhaps you might displace it onto someone else. Not what you want.

If you are on the receiving end of your boss's ire, as in the circumstance cited above, you have every right to be angry! And maybe you can't instantly fill your need for respect (if the boss is chronically unreasonable, filling that need might ultimately lead you to initiate a job search). But that's the point: by keeping your focus on filling the need, you get to decide which eventual choice will be the best one. By denying you are angry, nothing productive will be accomplished.

How do you know if you're angry and don't know it? After all, denial—by definition—means you are cut off from your own awareness. If you aren't sure, try the rundown of key questions on page 188.

The Danger of Displacement

When we are very angry at an unacceptable target—someone who intimidates us, who holds power over us, or who is in a position to hurt us—it is unwise and

Are You in Denial of Your Own Anger?

Could you be angrier than you think? One way to find out is to collect opinions from the (trusted) people around you. Yes, you can ask your mate and children: "Do I often seem angry?" If you are frequently being told (without asking), "You seem so angry," that's an important clue. Or perhaps you often catch yourself making remarks like these:

"I'm not angry—*you're* angry!"
"I wouldn't be angry if you didn't do . . ."
"I only get angry because you *tell* me I'm angry."
"I wouldn't be angry if you didn't keep insisting that I am!"

Next time someone makes the observation that you seem angry, try to use it as an opportunity to gather feedback. Ask some open-ended questions: "What makes you think that way? Is it something I do? Something I say? An expression on my face? Tone of voice?" Try to be open to the possibility that you may be angrier than you realize. Then seek to maximize rather than minimize the information you get from others: you may find it enlightening.

can even be perilous to express our anger. A far easier course is to take it out on someone less intimidating.

That, in essence, is what *displacement* is about. An illustrative anecdote describes how a disgruntled general would get angry at the colonel who gets angry at the major—and so on, all the way down the chain of command—to the private, who comes home and yells at his wife, who gets angry at the children, who in turn, kick the dog! When we displace our anger, we symbolically "kick the dog": that is, express rage not toward our *real* target but toward a far less threatening alternative.

Most of us have occasional incidents when we displace anger. Imagine, for instance, that you get pulled over for speeding; you don't tell off the police officer who hands you the ticket, but you *do* come home and immediately start snarling at your daughter when you notice she neglected to return a library book—because your daughter is, of course, an easier target for your rage. Displacement can become an *anger style*—a habitual way of handling angry feelings. That is an insidious pattern, an ingrained mode of behavior that can have damaging consequences.

Do you often catch yourself having irrational confrontations with your wife, son or daughter, a subordinate employee, salesclerks, or the teller at the bank? Maybe you sometimes hear the criticism, "Hey, I don't know what your problem is, but don't take it out on me!" If minor irritations seem to hook you disproportionately, consider the possibility that you may be displacing your anger. Ask yourself, *Am I really angry at my wife, my child, or the waiter?* Or is this hook actually coming from somewhere else? Part of good anger management is knowing how to identify and address the source of your anger—and then direct your response accordingly.

Doesn't the phenomenon of displacement indicate that anger was somehow "stored," metaphorically speaking, "awaiting an opportunity to seek expression," in keeping with Freud's theory of the aggressive drive and the hydraulic principle? The answer is no. Displaced anger is generally a matter of mood and usually occurs in temporal proximity to an angry event. Recall that anger is closely hardwired to the fight-or-flight response and that there is an increased survival benefit for a state of heightened arousal after a threat is perceived; i.e., the threat may be lurking nearby. At such times we are hypervigilant and have a biological predisposition to react with fight-or-flight.

So if you come home after an argument with a friend, or a confrontation with a supervisor or colleague at work, you will likely be primed to react to minor annoyances in keeping with your mood, lowering your threshold for yelling at your wife for forgetting to fill the gas tank or your children for leaving their clothes strewn all over the floor. And if one is in a job or central relationship characterized by chronic anger, the temptation to displace anger may occur in your life with great regularity.

If you are aware that you are in a bad mood, perhaps still angry over something that occurred a little while ago, it can be a big help: you will at least know that your "fuse has been shortened." Awareness is key! If possible, take some time to "chill out." Engage in any activity that restores your sense of calm. Suppress your impulse—*choose not to*—yell at your spouse, child, or subordinate. You will be glad you did.

Should You Discuss Your Anger with Others?

Many of the people I counsel ask whether talking about anger is a good idea. After all, they talk to me about it, so they wonder if talking to friends and family is as beneficial as talking to a psychotherapist. Will it help, or make matters worse?

The short answer is that it depends. On one hand, a sympathetic listener can help you get a clearer, more objective perspective on the situation. Someone you trust can give you unbiased feedback; he may spot things that you may not be well positioned to see. Let's say, hypothetically, that you are angry with your mother-in-law, and you tell a friend about it. Because this friend is not emotionally involved, he might be able to see the facts with greater clarity, letting you know if you may be personalizing the incident, taking it too seriously, or exaggerating its importance. In the words of the poet W. B. Yeats, someone who can "cast a cold eye" on things can be enormously helpful.

But there is also the danger that an outsider can help heat things up. It is entirely possible that sharing your anger with someone else will fan the flames of your rage and make you even angrier. Friends may relish pointing out all the other times your mother-in-law snubbed you (incidents that you might have long forgotten). They can stoke the coals of your anger instead of helping you reach a resolution.

Carole has a group of work friends who regularly have lunch together. At midday, six or seven women typically gather in the company conference room to eat and chat: "Since we're all in our twenties and thirties and most of us are married, we have a lot in common," Carole says. This lunchtime gabfest sometimes turns into a gripe session as the coworkers take turns lambasting their husbands, mothers-in-law, and so on. "I have to say that in one way, our talks felt therapeutic," Carole admits. "If I was having a day when I was really mad at my husband, it kind of helped to know I wasn't alone."

But in time, Carole began to see that the friends were giving each other too much negative reinforcement. Instead of arriving at solutions, they seemed to be creating an environment where anger intensified. "Sometimes it turned into a competitive sport to see who was the most put-upon," Carole says. "If I would complain about my husband, my friend Bobbie might say, 'You think that's bad? Wait till you hear what the jerk I'm married to did!' We seemed to be taking turns wallowing in our dissatisfaction instead of finding a way out of it."

Other people can be helpful—but they can also be harmful, particularly if they seem determined to fan the flames of your anger and prove that old adage, "Misery loves company." If you find the confidants you are talking to are making you angrier, it may be best to stop the discussion altogether. Or find confidants whose response will be constructive, rather than destructive, to your anger management goals.

A Matter of Expectations

There is another key way to manage anger more effectively: discover whether your unmet expectations are one of your own anger hooks. Then as you set out to identify and fill your own need, you may have to ask yourself another important question: *How realistic are my expectations?*

In the course of daily living, we all bring many expectations to the table. You expect the train will arrive on time, the coffee will be hot, the conference call will commence as scheduled, your spouse will pick up the dry cleaning as promised, and your son will remember to bring home the permission slip you have to sign. In short, you expect certain aspects of life to run in a more-or-less orderly and predictable fashion. Anytime those expectations are not met, there are grounds for anger.

Many times, of course, you are perfectly justified in being angry at failed expectations. If this is the fourth incident when the client hasn't been called as scheduled (respect) or your valuable time (territory) is being wasted by an individual who is chronically late . . . well, you certainly have to address the need for better compliance in the future.

But other times, we may have to give our own expectations a reality check. For instance: "I expect my child to get all A's on her report card"; "I expect my son to get a hit in every Little League game"; "I expect my wife to make love with me three times a week"; "I expect the trains to always run on time." Are these the kind of high standards you hold? If so, you might have to ask yourself if some of what you expect is unrealistic.

Any time you feel angry because a person or situation has "let you down," a difficult question needs to be asked (and answered honestly): is my expectation realistic or does it need to be reevaluated? By lowering the bar on unrealistic standards, we also lower the likelihood of becoming angry.

Three Important "Don'ts" of Anger Management

By now, if you have been putting some of the ideas of this book into practice, you probably have your own anger management track record. That is, you can point to times when you were successful at avoiding hooks; times when you inadvertently bit, but then managed to get the hook out of your mouth quickly as you set about filling your need; and times when you failed miserably at anger management despite your best intentions. If so, consider yourself right on track!

Effecting positive change is not easy. You may imagine it's a steady course, but more often it's a matter of the proverbial two steps forward, one step back. Whether we are seeking to lose weight, stop smoking, start running, or manage anger, the process of change is not easy. It's an arduous path laden with inevitable setbacks. That's one reason New Year's resolutions rarely work out: People get motivated and assume they will cure their ills once the clock strikes midnight. Then a few days or weeks later they have a weak moment—splurging on the chocolate cake or lighting up that cigarette—and the resolve disappears. They assume they're failures, so why bother to try anymore?

But when making changes, you have to give yourself credit for each victory rather than focus on the times you failed to hit the mark. One reason anger management is particularly challenging is the fact that anger clouds our judgment; once we are hooked, we are more likely to say or do things we will regret later. And from there, it's easy to feel as if we've failed: our motivation lags and our momentary sense of defeat can threaten to derail us altogether.

Be prepared for those moments! It helps to have a few guidelines to follow. That way, when you know your judgment is clouded you can follow these three helpful suggestions:

1. **Do not criticize when angry.** Many people have enormous difficulty being critiqued, especially when the criticism is laced with anger. Too often, even constructive criticism can be interpreted as a destructive attack. When criticized with an angry tone, people often react to the anger rather than the intended message. Typically, they become defensive and unable to hear potentially useful information about themselves. If a situation truly does warrant corrective measures, wait until the atmosphere is clear before saying anything critical. Like fine wine, criticism "goes down" best in a calm moment.

2. **Do not use abusive language or resort to physical attacks.** Words can sting, hurt, wound, and leave emotional scars that never completely heal. In therapy, some of the most painful incidents patients recount are times they were called disparaging names such as *worthless* or *moron*, or when they were blamed for a host of family ills. Any kind of hitting, slapping, or spanking is not acceptable: not only could it potentially cause injury, it inevitably breeds more and more anger. If you sense you are on the verge of becoming verbally or physically abusive, take a time-out. Quickly, definitively, right then and there.

3. **Do not threaten rejection or abandonment.** In the moment, you might honestly believe you don't ever want to lay eyes on someone again! But think how devastating such a statement can sound, particularly to a child. The fear of abandonment is one of the deepest terrors children have; to be threatened in this

way by the all-powerful parent (on whom the child depends for survival) is especially devastating. Adults, too, sometimes threaten to end a relationship in the heat of anger, maybe screaming "Get out now!" or "I want a divorce!" Such threats make a bad situation worse, compounding the difficulties in communication that are already occurring. Of course, furious people say all kinds of things they don't truly mean; sometimes in anger, we say the very thing that we know will hurt the most. But suggesting that someone will be rejected, abandoned, or never spoken to again . . . words like these cut very deep and can leave lasting scars.

Effective anger management may seem like a complicated list of dos and don'ts, tempered with much advice on when to "take time out" or "not go there." But the rewards of living in a thriving, happy family—where anger is managed in a healthy way—will be enormous.

New Beginnings:
Your "Optimal
Anger" Family

By now you may be wondering, what does the future look like once you've learned better ways to manage your anger? How does it feel to function—to laugh, work, play, pay bills, juggle chores, mourn losses, celebrate special occasions, and do all the other myriad things families do—in an "optimal anger" family?

Notice the key word here is *optimal*, as opposed to *perfect*. Optimal, by definition, means *the most desirable possible*. When we speak of an optimal return on investment, we mean the highest possible dividends, not boundless cash. In medical terms, an optimal course of treatment is the one that combines the greatest healing with the fewest side effects. It's the best we can reasonably do, even if it falls short of flawless.

Similarly, an "optimal anger" family is not a perpetually happy group that never experiences a trace of anger. Nor is it a family that always deals with anger in a fully functional, totally appropriate way. But it is a family—nuclear or extended—that strives to understand, manage, and express this often challenging emotion in the best way possible. Under optimal conditions, parents and children are committed to the goal of managing anger with an attitude of mutual respect. Clearly, that's a different—and much more attainable—mission than never getting angry at all.

Perhaps Aristotle expressed it best more than two thousand years ago: when any one of us is angry, the optimal choice is to express it "with the right person, to the right degree, at the right time, for the right purpose and in the right way." As we are all imperfect beings, this will never happen 100 percent of the time with any person—or in any family. But we can always work on boosting our success.

If you do have an anger-prone family, optimal anger inevitably means less anger. It also means that each family member is learning how to better contain his angry impulses and resolve them through open discussion and negotiation—not screaming, cursing, threatening, or physically lashing out. Ideally, each member is more adept at spotting his own personal anger hooks—without biting.

Back in Chapter 1, we learned that anger results from a failure in homeostasis; it can serve as an alerting mechanism that informs us when our needs are not being met. Rather than being a personal liability, anger is a natural, healthy, universal emotion—an important aspect of the human condition. Anger heightens our awareness, letting us know that something is in need of attention and, perhaps, in need of change; after all, if it weren't for our forebears' outrage at an unjust tax on tea, the United States might still be a British colony today.

In his book *The Road Less Traveled*, psychiatrist M. Scott Peck reflected on some key aspects of optimal anger:

> To function successfully in our complex world it is necessary for us to possess the capacity not only to express our anger but also not to express it. Moreover, we must possess the capacity to express our anger in different ways. At times, for instance, it is necessary to express it only after much deliberation and self-evaluation. At other times, it is more to our benefit to express it immediately and spontaneously. Sometimes it is best to express it coldly and calmly; at other times, loudly and hotly. . . . To handle our anger with full adequacy and competence, an elaborate, flexible response system is required.

Clearly, this is a complex, lifelong process that many of us never master completely. "Working on oneself," however, is a noble, rewarding goal. As the saying goes, "A life unexamined is not worth living."

Optimal Changes: An Angry Family Revisited

How would an "optimal anger" family—a family that has learned this three-step program, and now strives to manage anger with new adequacy and competence, react to some of the typical stresses of family life? One starting point might be to imagine an optimal version of the family profiled at the start of this book—Debbie and Paul and their two school-age children, Emily and Mark.

Things begin to go awry when Debbie comes home early on a Friday, harried from a long workweek but eagerly anticipating some time off. The first thing she hears upon entering the house is her mother's angry rantings on the answering machine, bearing news that Deb's father's driver's license has expired and Deb's chauffeuring services are needed. But instead of getting mad, Debbie steadies herself and says *hook!* Her mother's lack of consideration (injustice) and her father's oversight (incompetence) could readily hook her into getting angry. But instead, Deb says *need!* She realizes she has to address her own needs for respect and territory by deciding how much of her free time she can commit to her parents' welfare—and then calmly setting the appropriate limits. So now Deb focuses on the key question: how might she fill those needs?

She could take a brief time-out, vowing to call her mom in an hour or two (right now, she's afraid she might still bite the hook). When she does get in touch, Debbie could ask her mother, "What time is Dad's doctor's appointment? Because Mark has a soccer game tomorrow morning, and, I'm sorry, but I may not be available." If her mother protests, Debbie could say, "Mom, I'm happy to help when I can, but Saturday is my day off, a time when I make plans with my own family. With our hectic schedules, we hardly see one another all week. If you'd like, I can come over for an hour or so on Sunday to help you and Dad run errands. In the meantime, here's the number of a car service you can call to arrange transportation to the doctor tomorrow."

Debbie's tone is respectful but firm; if her mother counters with an outraged, "We need you! How can you be so selfish?" Deb might firmly reply, "Mom, I'm sorry I can't be there for you. I'll do what I can to help you find a solution—I just gave you the number of a car service—but until Dad gets his license back, this is the best I can do. I really do wish I could help out more, but I have other obligations that I must attend to."

Next, Debbie scans the mail and finds the unpaid bill and collection notice. Why, that irresponsible, incompetent . . . *hook!* Then immediately, *need*. Deb spots a respect need, a requirement that Paul keep her abreast of financial slipups since his actions affect the entire family. She is annoyed—no denying it—but how will she address it? Debbie takes a step back and reflects: "It's a collection notice—the bank isn't getting ready to repossess the car or the house." Debbie decides a brief planned discussion is in order; she will mention it to Paul tomorrow, when the atmosphere is more conducive to a calm dialogue. Perhaps they need a better system of keeping track of the bills.

Meanwhile, at his office, Paul is encountering his own set of anger hooks. The boss's insistence that he take work home is infringing on his free time (territory). Paul's anger also contains an underlying element of fear: he is insecure about a recent job error, nervous that he is being compared unfavorably to a colleague, and therefore particularly vulnerable to getting hooked. In this uneasy state, he might displace some of this anger onto Debbie and his children, since they pose far less potential danger than his cohorts at work.

But Paul has choices. Instead of biting the hook, he can assess his own need: to regain some (self-) respect so he will be better able to negotiate his job issues from a position of strength. Paul might think *It's not fair that I was put on this project, and I have a right to feel annoyed. But if I make the best of it—and do my best work* this time—*it's likely I'll regain some respect from my superiors, and I'll feel more valued. In the future, though, I'll try to hint that I would prefer being given a bit more notice.* (This is, of course, a touchy issue in the workplace these days.)

With this clear game plan in mind, and a vision of how to eventually meet his needs for respect and territory, Paul is in greater control. He is aware of his anger and no longer at the mercy of his angry impulses—nor is he likely to make Debbie and the children a target of his displaced anger.

At home, Debbie and Paul have a pleasant evening, unwinding with their two children and enjoying their time together. Instead of screaming and sarcasm, there is laughter and warm interaction; instead of retreating to their bedrooms to avoid hearing their parents' fight, Emily and Mark hang out in the den, where the biggest argument centers on who gets to pick the TV show. Are things perfect? Not entirely: Paul and Debbie still have to have that financial discussion; Paul has the weekend workload looming; and Debbie will likely spend at least an hour on Sunday taking her parents grocery shopping. But these minor challenges— these potential anger hooks—are being managed in a calm and tactical way. Needs are being met with more flexibility, more control, and much less anger.

A Flexible Response System: Anger Management in a Nutshell

Here is a brief, succinct version of the program presented in this book: think of it as a handy reference guide to be used anytime you find yourself needing a quick anger management refresher course.

- **Definition of anger.** Developmentally, anger is a natural reaction to a failure in homeostasis (an organism's tendency to maintain stable biological conditions). We humans often feel angry whenever we perceive a threat to our physical or psychological well-being.
- **The advantage of anger.** Much like pain and fear, anger serves as a kind of psychological warning device—anger tells us that we feel something is wrong and merits our attention. From a biological standpoint, anger is a sign that homeostasis has been disturbed and a need must be filled.
- **The way we express anger.** While we may all experience anger, we learn to manage it differently—often imitating behavior we observed in our same-sex parent. Some manage anger without apparent difficulty. Others scream and yell. Some appear calm, but seethe inwardly. Others turn passive-aggressive. By adulthood, we have all developed characteristic ways of managing anger-provoking situations—in short, our method of expressing anger becomes a matter of *character*.
- **One of the biggest misconceptions about anger.** Many of us envision anger as "something"—akin to a substance—that accumulates and requires a release. This is a common misconception likely based on Freud's understanding of the aggressive drive. Many people

believe they must express their anger (in other words, rant and rave) or there will be disastrous consequences later on.

Anger does not "build up"—it gets reactivated. It does not accumulate inside of us. Instead, it may seem to increase if we are repeatedly exposed to the same anger-provoking event. Sometimes we provide our own repeated exposure by replaying anger-provoking experiences in our minds. That's one reason it may feel as if anger is building.

If we believe we *must* express our anger—that it will continue to build until we are ready to explode—we fail to see other options for managing anger effectively. The truth is, we don't have to *react* in anger: we can choose an optimal way to *respond* instead. This key point is crucial for successful anger management.

A Three-Step Plan for Optimal Anger Management

Step One: Identify the Hook

- The "hook" is a metaphor for the "lures" that trigger anger; as we move through the sea of life many hooks—that is, good reasons to get angry—will drop down before us.
- Most hooks fall into two categories: we get angry at circumstances that reflect *injustice*

(actions that are unfair, immoral, selfish, and so on) and *incompetence* (anything or anyone we deem inept, lazy, or stupid).

- To help you become more adept at spotting hooks, begin a Hook Book. Write down each time you get angry and describe the event, noting whether each particular anger hook derives from some display of injustice or incompetence. As you review each event, ask yourself, *Who or what was involved? How did I feel? How did I* react? *How might I have* responded, *instead?*

Step Two: Identify the Need

- Recognize that we generally become angry whenever a need is frustrated: if you look beyond the injustice or incompetence hooks, it's likely you will discover an unmet need.
- Biological needs include food, shelter, rest and sleep, and a comfortable temperature.
- The two generally unrecognized psychological needs most frequently embedded in anger-provoking events are for *respect* and *territory*.
- Our *respect* is violated when others do not try to understand us, fail to keep promises, make decisions without our permission, impose their values on us, make negative or abusive remarks, lie, and so on.
- Our *territory* (or turf) is "trampled" whenever someone takes our belongings, makes too

many demands on our time, gets too close,
wants too much intimacy, bombards us with
loud music or other noise, or otherwise
encroaches on our personal space.
- Whenever you become angry, ask yourself,
*Which need is not filled? A biological need?
Hunger, shelter, rest, sleep, temperature? My
need for respect? My need for territory?*

Step Three: Fill the Need
- Whenever you encounter a hook and identify
your need, figure out how to substitute a *need-fulfillment response* for your *angry reaction.*
Discover how you can meet your needs for
respect, for territory, or both.
- As you set out to fill that need, ask yourself,
*What goal am I trying to achieve? What outcome
do I want?*

Optimal Strategies: The Value of Open Discussion

Getting your needs met involves a number of different strategies—and as Peck noted, having the capacity "not only to express our anger but also not to express it" is a skill worth cultivating. Families, in particular, will benefit from knowing how to address their everyday conflicts without hooking one another.

When it comes to resolving conflict, *open discussion* is one smart tactic because it offers two big advantages. First, the ability to sit down and calmly resolve disagreements makes family life more pleasant and civil; it helps keep the hooks to a minimum. When children sense they are being heard, they are less likely to shout or express their dissent with bad behavior. Similarly, when parents feel they can communicate clearly—and that their children are being receptive, if not totally compliant—they too are less likely to succumb to their old angry ways.

Second, open discussion shows our children a *respectful* way to deal with conflict. When we can discuss rather than yell, we model good anger management skills, giving our children lessons in how to constructively resolve life's inevitable disagreements.

Here is an example of an open discussion in my own family. My twelve-year-old daughter likes to play video games, a typical pursuit for a girl her age. But since she is also a gymnast, she requires sufficient rest in order to perform well without risking injury. The need to balance a suitable bedtime with a sufficient amount of leisure time can become quite a conflict.

When my wife and I go into our daughter's room close to bedtime and see her riveted to the computer, we start by asking her what time she plans to go to bed (showing some respect for her turf, her ability to manage her own schedule). She cites a time, but often continues playing beyond the hour she specified for bed. If she cajoles us for "just five more minutes" we will often bend. But beyond a certain point, my wife and I "draw a line in the sand" *together.*

Parental togetherness is key. Children learn early on how to "split" their parents, asking the other after the first says no. We might say, "You will lose a certain amount of time from gymnastics if you continue to play on the computer. *You* said you wanted to be in bed by such-and-such a time."

Instead of getting angry, we provide a framework for our daughter to manage not just her schedule but her own conflicting desires. At the same time, we stand firm—as parents should—demonstrating to our daughter that her actions have consequences. So far, this technique has worked; we have yet to penalize our daughter. And few angry words have been exchanged. That's one example of an "optimal anger" solution.

Of course, family issues are often much more complex than the simple matter of negotiating a bedtime. Bitter fights and ancient grudges, unresolved conflicts and ongoing competition, difficult personalities . . . all these can add extra resonance to even minor anger disputes. How do you arrive at healthy solutions if old wounds have festered, or if family members have allowed so much time and distance to elapse that problems seem insurmountable? (Or, as one of my patients put it, "What do you do if those hooks have turned rusty?!")

It may not be easy to arrive at optimal anger solutions, but it is almost always possible to make a bad situation better. If you can master these basic tools of anger management—spotting and avoiding the hook, identifying the need, and finding a way to get that need filled—you are well on your way to handling problem situations with less anger and more understanding. Let's look at just a few common circumstances you might face, and what may be required to arrive at optimal (if not perfect) resolutions.

Four Steps to Conflict Resolution

The same principles that apply to labor disputes and other kinds of mediation can help you negotiate a host of family issues.

1. **State your position.** Make a clear, calm statement of how things look from your viewpoint.
2. **State your opponent's position.** Make a similar statement, but this time imagine you are seeing things from the other party's perspective. Mirror what he or she may be feeling, thinking, or wanting.
3. **Present a proposal for solving the problem.** Put an "offer on the table"—some resolution that is acceptable to both you and your

opponent, and one that will meet both your needs.

4. **Make an agreement.** Agree to the new terms—perhaps even spelling out the particulars by putting the fine points in writing. Accept the resolution and abide by it.

When resolving any conflict, it helps to have some psychic distance from the matter at hand, particularly if it is a hot-button issue. You must also be prepared to give in a bit: successful resolution often entails some compromise on both sides. But compromise shows an admirable flexibility, along with respect for your opponent. And respect—as we now know—helps keep the anger away!

A Common Family Turf Battle: When Grandparents Interfere with Grandchildren

When adult children have children of their own, it sometimes sets the stage for a complex three-generation dynamic: many sensitive "turf" issues can emerge between grandparents, parents, and children. If the family has always grappled with anger issues—or if many anger-provoking matters have been left unresolved—there can be a number of old and new hooks with tasty-looking bait, just waiting to drop down in front of you.

First, let's look at things from the perspective of the older generation. For some, the experience of becoming a grandparent is thrilling: "It's like having your own children all over again, but this time there's less stress." Others may think, *Oh, no . . . I'm not ready to be a grandparent!* The very idea may force individuals to confront uncomfortable notions of aging, the realization that one's own youth (and perhaps power) is slipping away. Instead, adult children are the ones entering their prime; they're now parents in their own right.

Grandparents can react to these issues in a variety of ways. Some may develop an excessive preoccupation with grandchildren, vying for the little one's attention and perhaps competing to "outdo" the parent, their own adult child. Other grandmothers and grandfathers slip naturally into the authoritative role: "We know best!" they might declare to their adult children who have more recently become parents. "After all, we raised you, didn't we?" To which the adult child—remembering angry scenes from his own youth—may think, "You raised me, all right . . . and I'm going to make sure you don't get a chance to make the same mistakes with my children!"

The experience of becoming a parent often stirs up memories of one's own childhood; it stimulates you to relive some of the pain and anxiety you felt growing up. If you were often the target of your mother's or father's anger, it may be excruciatingly painful to imagine your own child victimized in much the same way. Any time you see your mother or father lose patience with *your* child—maybe using words like *crybaby* or saying "Can't you do anything right?" to a three-year-old—it can easily bring back everything you felt as a helpless, dependent, and frightened youngster. What appealing anger bait that can be!

"One of the first times I ever really confronted my mother was over a nasty remark she made to my child," Linda recalls. Ever the compliant daughter, Linda had always been overly timid around her mother, an overbearing woman who used anger to browbeat her family and get her own way. That is, until Linda's child became involved.

Linda recalls, "My mother and I were supposed to take my four-year-old daughter out to lunch, and my mother was furious that I had the 'wrong outfit' on her—apparently it wasn't frilly or expensive enough. She started yelling at me, 'How do you expect me to take her out looking like that?' But my daughter thought that *she* had done something wrong. I remember the pained look on her face as she started to cry, and I was *livid*. I screamed at my mother, 'How dare you! Don't you realize how terrible that sounds, coming from a grandparent? It's like you're saying she's 'not good enough' just because of what she's wearing. Newsflash, Mom . . . we're not as shallow as you are, judging people by how they dress!' "

Clearly, Linda had bitten the hook: she had become enraged when her mother showed disrespect for her child. She realized, in short order, that the most crucial task was to restore that respect, to make sure that she and her daughter were not left wounded by her mother's inappropriate comments. "So I sat my daughter down and said, 'I'm sorry Grammie hurt your feelings. She sees things a bit differently than we do—when she was a little girl, people would get really dressed up when they went out. To me, that seems kind of silly. But sometimes grownups disagree about things like that. And actually, Grammie was angry at me, not you.'" Not a perfect solution, Linda realizes, but "at least it's better than having my daughter come away feeling badly about herself, the way I always did when my mother made cutting remarks to me."

At the same time, Linda has made it clear to her mother that these kinds of remarks to Linda's child will not be permitted. "I realize that it's my job to ensure that my daughter is respected; it's *not* my job to do my mother's bidding," Linda said. "As for the decisions on how my daughter is raised . . . that's my turf."

Then there is the view from the *other* side of the generational divide: what is the "optimal" approach when you see your adult children displaying undue anger toward your grandchildren? Jason, a sixtyish widower, went to spend a few days with his divorced daughter Stephanie and his four-year-old grandson,

Alex, whom he adored. One evening, in a restaurant, Jason struggled hard not to say a word as Stephanie struggled even harder to get Alex into his seat for dinner. Finally, Stephanie picked up Alex and forcefully pushed him down on the chair, yelling, "Sit there, or else!" Jason was shocked, but then he made what he thought was a helpful comment: "Perhaps it would work better if you didn't make such a big issue out of it." Indignant about her father's interference, Stephanie shot back, "Butt out! You're undermining my authority." The rest of the evening and all the next day were glum, as Stephanie and her dad scarcely said a word to one another.

Another patient, Barbara, is anguished over her adult children who don't believe in setting too many limits early in their child's development. One time Barbara's daughter was offended when Barbara taught her granddaughter how to hold a fork properly. "How dare she tell my child what to do while she's a guest in my house?" noted the indignant daughter. Barbara confided, "I was only trying to be helpful."

Clearly, Barbara's motives—and Jason's—may be good: they are "only trying to help." But trying to be helpful on someone else's turf can be a very sensitive issue. Despite your good intentions, your words may be construed as judgmental or interfering—a potent anger hook that your adult child is apt to bite.

Not all anger issues have neat-and-pretty solutions. Sometimes a "good-enough" resolution will have to suffice. For Jason, Barbara, and Linda, the pivotal question isn't *Who's right about the matter at hand?* but *Whose territory is it, anyway?* Realizing where the boundaries are—recognizing when you're about to trample on someone else's turf—can be invaluable. It isn't always easy to hold your tongue and resist intervening, especially when you really do have a grandchild's best interest at heart—not to mention a great deal of life experience. (And of course, if problems are very serious—if a child is being subjected to physical or verbal lashings, substance abuse, or neglect—a grandparent may well have an obligation to step in. Even the court considers child abuse matters its rightful "territory," and professionals in schools, the medical community, and elsewhere are mandated by law to report suspicions of child endangerment.) But matters of dress, etiquette, and limit-setting just aren't worth biting the anger hook!

The Final Stage of Anger Management: Knowing When to Let Go

If managing anger entails filling a need, and if filling that need means asking *What are my goals?* and *What outcome do I want?* . . . what happens when you realize your best possible outcome is an impossibility?

That is another key aspect of arriving at optimal solutions: recognizing when issues will never be fully resolved and realizing that your needs will not always be filled. It's a hallmark of maturity to accept other people's limitations—to recognize that you may never have the warm, loving relationship with a parent that you wish you could, or to realize that some rifts or old grudges may never be resolved to your satisfaction. Instead of continually being hooked and rehooked by these ongoing anger issues, it is best to know when to swim around them. In an optimal anger family, members know when to let things go.

Minimizing the Anger Hooks After a Divorce

When people speak of an "amicable divorce," that too is an optimal response to a less-than-perfect circumstance. Even in the best of situations, a broken marriage is a painful experience for all involved. Loss, guilt, sadness, painful feelings, a sense of betrayal, financial hardship, the assortment of stresses on children . . . clearly, there is no shortage of good reasons to get angry when a marriage ends.

Divorce seems to inevitably entail the two "I"s that categorize most anger hooks: injustice and incompetence. If the split-up was marked by infidelity, the wronged spouse may be overcome with the unfairness of the circumstance, by what he or she perceives as a huge miscarriage of justice. If the final days of the marriage entailed lots of fighting and name-calling—and children were uneasy witnesses to those events—their sense of security may be eroded. It's upsetting to watch two people you love and depend on behaving in such an angry, unpredictable manner. Children may well think, *Why can't the two of you stop fighting and take care of us?* If children are asked to take sides, or if former spouses each try to win the child's favor at the other parent's expense, it can leave a host of bad feelings all around. Divorce is notorious for leaving a great many unresolved anger issues in its wake.

There's an old adage that time heals all wounds, but studies show that that isn't always the case for divorced spouses and their offspring. Judith Wallerstein, a foremost expert who has conducted several studies on how divorce affects children, says it is disturbingly common for former spouses to stay angry at one another—and that anger continues to impact the children. "In our study, a third of the [divorced] couples were fighting at the same high pitch ten years after the divorce was final," she writes in *The Unexpected Legacy of Divorce: A Twenty-Five-Year Landmark Study.* "Their enduring anger stemmed from continuous feelings of hurt and humiliation fueled by new complaints (child support is too burdensome or too little) and jealousy over new, often younger partners. The notion that divorce ends the intense love/hate relationship of a marriage is another myth. . . . Millions of children today experience the . . . unrelenting drama of longing and anger that refuses to die." Even after a marriage ends, the anger hooks often keep on coming.

Few would argue that Lizzie had reason to be bitter and furious with her ex-husband David. She had tried to do everything right throughout the couple's twelve-year marriage—making a home, raising four children, and otherwise being the "ideal" wife. But their relationship had been impacted by David's drug use, his rages (including an incident where he threw their eight-year-old down half a flight of stairs), and his infidelities. One day, David announced he was leaving Lizzie—and their children, who were four, six, eight, and ten at the time—so he could move in with Lizzie's best friend. "I was shocked, furious, speechless . . . I mean, that bastard!" Years later, Lizzie can still recall the outrage as if it happened yesterday.

And in the throes of early divorce, Lizzie responded by letting everyone—her lawyer, her children, her family and friends, even casual acquaintances—hear her tirade of fury against her former spouse. Things went from bad to worse, and Lizzie went from angry to angrier as the catalog of grievances grew: David was late with a child-support payment. He left the children with a fourteen-year-old babysitter (a caretaker Lizzie deemed too young) during a weekend visitation. Instead of taking the children on a spring break vacation as promised, he pleaded a busy schedule but then managed a long weekend with his live-in girlfriend. Lizzie self-righteously aired the details of each of these injustices to anyone who would listen—including her four children.

But this anger, however justified, wasn't helping this wounded family move on to a healthier place.

Instead, the household was in a state of chronic angst and ill-disguised fury. The children fought constantly; school psychologists told Lizzie they were "acting out." Her six-year-old daughter began to have nightmares. The ten-year-old son, the oldest, began to lose interest in friends and the soccer games he normally loved. Lizzie gradually came to realize that something had to change. "Maybe I had a right to be angry at David, but it wasn't right to make the kids suffer for it."

As long as she kept biting incessantly into the anger hooks, Lizzie was refueling her own rage. It took time and resolve for her to focus on filling the underlying need instead. "For a while, I had trouble getting past the idea that I was getting so little *respect* from David," Lizzie admits. "And I guess a lot of that was the tremendous anger I felt over the shabby way I'd been treated. But when I began to focus on the need for territory, I started to realize that maybe it was my job to create that new turf: a peaceful home where my kids could feel safe and happy, without all that anger."

Visualizing things in this way gave Lizzie a sense of empowerment, and that, in turn, helped combat some of the helplessness she felt over her circumstances. She made a vow to deal with her ex-husband as civilly as possible, trying not to bite the anger hooks he dropped in her path. Gradually, with the children's welfare in mind, Lizzie was able to take the steps needed to move from victim to victor over her anger.

Carol Tavris writes that there is "a moral as well as a psychological reason for managing anger after divorce and for eventually resolving it: to protect one's children as well as oneself." When mothers and fathers are able to put their differences aside—when they can avoid dropping and biting into the predictable batch of post-divorce anger hooks—they are doing something vitally important to help their children move forward with confidence and success.

Shawn is a twenty-six-year-old whose parents divorced when he was eight. Though it was hardly an ideal situation, Shawn says, "My parents really did do the best they could to make it easy for my sister and me." He recalls, "They didn't bicker in front of us, and actually seemed to present a united front whenever any parenting issue had to be resolved." Though he lived with his mom, Shawn always had regular visits with his dad. "They also were pretty involved in the things we did and managed to be friendly enough to each other when it came to things like our school recitals or games."

Most important, Shawn's parents avoided the trap—or hook—of letting their own anger get out of control; whatever their differences, they did not use the children as sounding boards or scapegoats. It wasn't perfect, Shawn recalls; he and his sister felt regret that the split had occurred, and they did experience the inevitable sadness ("Holidays were tough") as well as some challenging adjustments to new relationships and eventually, to stepparents. But he sensed the ongoing love, and the wish to do the right thing, that motivated his parents' behavior. According to

Judith Wallerstein, when parents are able to do this, they "will be providing an example of moral behavior in which every family member receives full consideration . . . [Children] will learn that parents in crisis can be trusted not to disappear but to be reliable and available as before, perhaps even more so." It represents an optimal approach, if not necessarily a perfect solution.

The anger in families that have been split by divorce is easy to understand. It isn't really surprising that the ex-spouses are angry at each other, or that the children are angry at their parents for creating this less-than-ideal situation. But, of course, anger is also passed on in families that stay together. Perhaps they are not always as nice to each other as they could be, but they are together nonetheless.

Brian has always prided himself on being an optimist. Though he grew up in a complex, volatile family—with a number of different anger styles, and many angry clashes—he always held firm to the belief "We've got to see the good in each other, not just the bad." Perhaps it was this inborn conviction that led Brian to his chosen profession as a marital mediator. In many of the anecdotes he shares about his own formative years, it's evident he had a knack for finding creative ways around his family's anger hooks.

"My mother could be very manipulative—she had a way of playing us off against each other and trying to get us to take sides," Brian recalls. One time, when she had an explosive argument with Brian's older sister, she called Brian to sound off. "She went on and on about how my sister Patty was so unreasonable and how she had said so many hurtful things," Brian recalls. "Patty definitely has her issues. But I tried to calm my mother down by saying she probably didn't mean any harm, how she had her own stresses and often flies off the handle."

Furious that Brian had failed to join in the Patty-bashing, his mother tossed out a new hook: "I can't believe you could defend your sister; you should hear all the awful things she says about *you.*" To which Brian calmly replied, "Mom, if I took everything everyone said as seriously as you do, I would have stopped talking to half the family somewhere around the late 1980s. So let's not blow this out of proportion."

Today, Brian recognizes that he just has to let certain things go. "There were plenty of times when I've been hurt by my parents and by some of the nasty things said in our house." His father was always a stern taskmaster; frequently, Brian and his siblings felt they couldn't reason with their dad, couldn't make him understand their needs. "You couldn't reason with my dad. It was his way or no way!" But Brian has come to see a softer side to his father and to understand some of the demons that shaped his early life. "I think my father really did love us, even if he sometimes showed more anger than affection," he says. "Truthfully, he himself had a very tough upbringing with his own angry father, so that must have affected him. And back in his day, people weren't as introspective as they are today. He probably just automatically parented us the way his father parented him. If I even try to *picture* my dad getting in touch with his feelings—well, I really can't picture it at all!"

One way Brian helps his own outlook is to affirm his (now deceased) father as "more good than bad." Without denying some of his old painful memories, he chooses to focus on the positive experiences instead. "Once when my own son was just a year old, he accidentally rolled off a changing table and broke his leg. Luckily he healed quickly, but my wife and I felt *awful*, like we were the worst parents imaginable," Brian recalls. "But a few days after it happened, I got this very kind and very unexpected letter from my father. Since he had a medical background, he started by assuring me that my son would be fine. He wrote, 'The worst part is probably how much this whole episode has upset you.' Then he enclosed a newspaper clipping about a child with a much more serious ailment—cystic fibrosis, I think—and ended by saying, 'Hopefully this will help keep things in perspective.' At a moment when I was having serious doubts about what kind of father I was, my own father made me feel better."

Brian goes on to say, "Sure, I could also recall all the times my father blamed me unfairly for things, shouted at me, or told me I'd never amount to anything. I'm not trying to paint this idyllic picture of how things were. But it's just much more comforting to remember the positive things about both my parents. It brings things to a more peaceful sense of closure."

Brian has learned to understand, forgive, let go, and move on. He says philosophically, "I learned a lot from my parents, but not necessarily what they intended to teach me." He realizes he will never resolve all his anger issues with his parents; some of his needs for respect and understanding will have never been met. But Brian is also keeping his focus on the most important outcome: he recognizes he has the power and knowledge to do better with his own children.

Experts believe that the way anger is managed has an enormous impact on emotional well-being. A position statement released by the American Psychological Association says, "Chronic unresolved conflict is associated with greater emotional insecurity in children. Fear, distress, and other symptoms in children are diminished when parents resolve their conflicts and when they use compromise and negotiation methods rather than verbal attacks. The beneficial effects of these more resolution-oriented behaviors have been reported whether or not they are directly observed by the child." Although this statement was devised for children of divorce, it clearly applies to all children.

The "Three A's" of Dealing with Stress

No matter how well you learn to manage your anger, difficult circumstances will befall you. Psychologist

Carl E. Thoresen of Stanford University notes that when it comes to managing stressful situations we have only three possible options. We can:

- **Avoid** the stressor: for instance, by choosing to travel when there is little traffic, if that is a major source of your discomfort. We will never be able to avoid all of life's stressors, however.
- **Alter** the stressor. However, be prepared to expend considerable time and energy. Imagine how difficult it would be to "fix" traffic or a hostile coworker. I recall a gentleman who approached me after an anger and stress management seminar I had just conducted. He appeared quite agitated as he exclaimed, "I registered for the wrong course. I want the one where you learn how to change other people!" There is no such course. We can only change ourselves, and then only with considerable effort.
- **Adjust** to the stressful situation. This is frequently our best option. After appearing on a television news show to talk about how to manage stress in traffic, the next day I found myself, with my mother, wife, and daughter, traveling to a niece's out-of-town college graduation. As we approached one of the tunnels leading out of the city, we traveled all of one block in an hour. There was no escape, noth-

ing I could do other than what I had advised on TV the day before: adjust as best you can. We talked among ourselves; I practiced deep breathing and listened to some music. It was still unpleasant being stuck in that traffic, but I managed to make an "optimal" adjustment. Looking back on that day, the events scarcely affect me, except as a lesson in how to deal with one of life's inevitable adversities.

Anger does not have to be an indelible family legacy: parents and children *can* break the cycle—can succeed in creating an atmosphere where there is a more reasoned approach to conflict resolution, greater mutual respect, fewer hooks, and less anger. And less anger invariably means more happiness.

Epilogue

So, after those three dreadful words spoken by my psychotherapy supervisor, "You sound cruel," and all these years, what has an exhaustive study of anger and its management done for me? My twelve-year-old daughter gave me a B. When asked for a grade, my wife abstained. Gentle soul that she is, I have had to teach her how to argue. Once when we were in Japan, she was selecting a robe to bring back as a gift for her mother. "Why are you buying her a robe?" I challenged. "You know she never likes anything you give her." My wife didn't say a word and I realized she needed help expressing herself—so I took her side in the argument. "You want to, that's why. Even if she doesn't like it, you still want to bring her a present. She's your mother." And so, by taking my wife's side in the argument, I helped her learn how to assert herself more effectively. (Angry men often marry soft-spoken, understanding women as a kind of counterbalance.)

In truth, I am still haunted by many angry thoughts and feelings. I have a passion for both fairness and excellence, and anything less still evokes a reaction—usually at least a twinge of annoyance. Injustice and incompetence are all around. However, rarely do I give in to my impulses to "teach someone a lesson." I know it won't do any good. Instead, I keep my anger to myself—nearly all of the time.

Anger-provoking situations require sensitivity and diplomacy for their resolution. These are traits that are difficult to tap into when angry. So, I wait. Much of the time, the situation seems to resolve itself, or it no longer looms so important later on. When an issue does require discussion, I do my best to choose an opportune moment to bring it up. While not always easy, this has clearly been my "optimal" path for resolving conflict.

In Search of the "Holy Grail"

Writing this book has been an intellectual challenge, and some of my ideas about anger have evolved over the two years it has taken to complete the project. I was pleased that I kept my cool and didn't get angry during the following recent odyssey.

My research on the relationship between anger, the aggressive drive, and the hydraulic principle led me to speak with Dr. George Makari, a colleague at Cornell, a modern-day psychoanalyst and expert in the history of Freud's ideas. Dr. Makari suggested I track down a slim volume published in 1965, *Freud's Neurological Education*, by Peter Amacher.

I looked through the catalog in the Weill Cornell Medical Library and there it was. However, when I arrived at the shelf with the specified call numbers, there was no book. I spoke to the librarian and was informed that the book was at the Rockefeller Library, where we have privileges. The next day I eagerly made my way over to the Rockefeller Library where, lo and behold, there was no book either. "I made the same mistake when I interviewed for my job," the cheerful librarian confided. "This is the Rockefeller Library at Memorial Sloan Kettering Hospital. You want the library across the street at Rockefeller University."

Undaunted, I trudged a few more blocks, on a cold and windy day, over to the august Rockefeller University—up a steep hill and into the imposing Founders Hall, where a guard asked for my ID. With a quick glance he said, "You don't have a bar code. You have to go back to the Cornell library to get one." And so back out into the cold I trudged three more blocks, obtained my bar code, and made my way back to the Rockefeller University library, where I finally gained entrance.

It was a huge, cavernous, and dusky place, but I eventually found my way to a woman who was sitting behind what looked like bulletproof glass. She took my ID and asked if I was logged into the system. I suggested that perhaps she might log me in while I had a look for the book. Quite agreeable, she directed me down a narrow staircase that appeared to be leading to a dungeon. At the bottom of the stairs, I came upon a large room where daylight shone through onto a long row of books. I soon came upon the precious volume I had been seeking alongside several books by former professors at New York University, where I had studied psychoanalytic theory many years before.

As I walked back up the dank stairwell, proudly clutching my "grail," I quickly discovered that all the doors were locked, except for one that was alarmed. "Must I set off an alarm to get out of here?" I wondered. As I looked around, I saw an ancient elevator nearby and got in. This was the kind of elevator that was formerly manned; it had a heavy iron gate behind the door, which I eventually figured out how to maneuver. There was no indication of which button to push to get back to the main library, however. I selected a button and beginner's luck had me exit near the dusky room where I had left my ID. Indeed, I was registered and, yes, I could take the book out for two weeks!

Victorious, I reclaimed my ID and strode out the library door, clutching my prize—when an alarm went off. The guard at the desk told me that I had to go upstairs to the main librarian and check out the book again, as it had set off the alarm. Within thirty seconds the head librarian appeared and offered to take the book upstairs to check it out herself. Three minutes later I was finally on my way.

Throughout this odyssey, I did not get angry. Rather, I was amazed at how many things could go wrong. I was also pleased by how well I had practiced what I preach.

Transforming Adversity to Advantage

Another incident reminds me of how, on some occasions, anger management has really paid off. I share the following as an example of an anger management success story.

My wife, daughter, and I arrived exhausted for our brief winter vacation in Orlando. Up at 5 A.M., after puttering around the night before until well after midnight, we had taken an 8 A.M. flight from New York City in order to spend most of the day in Florida. All of us were tired from demanding work and school schedules, my daughter's five-day-a-week after-school gymnastics program, and last-minute preparations for the trip.

After arriving at our hotel, with which I had been impressed when I had given an anger management lecture there about a dozen years before, we were shown to a dreary room overlooking a swamp. "Could we possibly have a different room?" I inquired. We were quickly whisked away to a brighter, more attractive room on a high floor with an expansive view of central Florida. ("If you don't ask, you don't get," I thought to myself. "Fill your need! Get what you want!") Quite contented, my family and I rode the elevator down to the pool where we lay in the warm sun, like limp noodles stretched across chaise longues, for the remainder of the afternoon. New York had been cold; we were exhausted and the warmth and sunshine felt great. We had previously decided to have dinner in the hotel so that we could go to sleep early and— biggest luxury of all—set no alarm clocks.

Dinner was just awful! My wife's crab cakes were greasy and salty, my daughter's pasta was smothered in sour-tasting tomato sauce far worse than anything served for lunch at her school, and my expensive salad was skimpy and totally nondescript. It seemed to me that the only thing that has changed about hotel food over the years was the elaborate description now given to the ingredients: "fresh jumbo Maryland crabmeat exquisitely sautéed by our master chef," "pasta (no longer spaghetti) in our award-winning homemade marinara sauce," and the chef's "special salad"— mostly iceberg lettuce, served with an oily vinaigrette. Defeated, we retired to our room and were soundly asleep before 10 P.M. None of us could remember having gone to bed so early.

The next morning, the sound of buzzing machinery rudely awakened us at 9 A.M. When we had arrived, there was a note in the room apologizing for any inconvenience from "necessary work" on the building's exterior that was being done from 9 to 5. Just our luck! Brick pointing on our New York City apartment building had also been going on for months. The noise, like a loud swarm of buzzing bees, just festered and wouldn't go away. It totally ruined our quietude and soured our moods this first morning of the vacation. Quite annoyed, I called the front desk to ask if something might be done. Within a few minutes, a friendly and apologetic woman appeared at our door. She graciously offered us a room in a different section of the hotel where we would not be disturbed.

The new room, smaller and on a lower floor than the one we had first rejected, had the same ugly swamp view. And the sound of the buzzing was nearly as loud as the room in which we had just spent the night. As I looked around, I noticed that there was no bed for my daughter. A "roll-away" would be brought in, the delegate from guest services offered. "But I paid extra for a 'superior' room to make sure that my daughter had a proper bed," I exclaimed as I started to come unglued. "Are you going to charge me the same price for a smaller room without a second bed?" I asked. "Since you booked your room as part of a package, there's nothing I can do," the woman apologized.

What an outrage! I thought of complaining to the Internet tourist agency that booked our trip. My mind was flooded with fantasies of checking out and finding a new hotel. I quickly realized, however, what an enormous inconvenience that would become. We would spend our precious vacation hours on the phone, probably on hold for much of the time, and then have to repack our bags, check into another hotel, and unpack all over again. And there was no guarantee that we would fare any better in a different hotel. At the very least, we would lose a good part of the day.

"Anger management," I thought, "that's what you do for a living. When you are angry, discover the 'hook' (that was easy) and fill your need. You need a decent room without buzzing machines to ruin your peace and quiet," I told myself. Still indignant, I headed downstairs to find the hotel manager.

"The manager is not in," said the receptionist in the Executive Office suite. "His secretary may be able to help you, though." JoAnne and I met midway between Reception and her office, as I had indeed lost my composure and started charging down the hall. "I can't tell you what a terrible time we've had since checking into this hotel yesterday," I exclaimed. "I'm sorry I'm so angry, but this has just been an awful experience."

After asking me to have a seat in her office, sympathetic and "all ears," JoAnne registered my complaints. She apologized for the unsatisfactory dinner and offered to take care of the bill. After she heard about the problem with the room, she said, "I am so sorry about the awful experiences you have had here. It's really not our way at all. Dr. Allan, we would like to offer you and your family the Presidential Suite for the rest of your stay, at the same rate you are now paying. It's our best room and I'm sure that you and your family will enjoy it. The suite comes with complimentary breakfast, snacks at tea time, and dessert after dinner, as well as a free membership in the health club. I'm so sorry you've had such a difficult time. I hope this will make it up to you."

I soon joined my wife and daughter in our duplex Presidential Suite, with twenty-five-foot floor-to-ceiling windows looking out onto an expansive view of central Florida. There was a living room, dining room, separate bedroom for my daughter, and a Jacuzzi and television in each of the marble bathrooms. My anger quickly abated as our vacation truly got under way.

Notice, from this example, that I did not raise my voice at anyone. (Well, maybe my tone was a bit surly after I was told the manager was not in.) I even apologized for my anger, realizing how unpleasant it can be. I also did not ask for anything. I gave up control to another person by sharing my feelings and asking for help. While there is no guarantee that help will always be forthcoming (indeed, in some circumstances it will not), when told of another's unhappiness most people do want to help—and they will if they can. The woman from Guest Services did not have the authority to offer us more than she did. As one moves up the chain of command in any organization, however, options generally increase. As a rule of thumb, it's best to deal with problems with the most senior person available.

So this initially unhappy experience was transformed into a successful case of anger management. A win-win for all involved. If we return to Orlando, my family and I might well check into that same hotel. And we certainly enjoyed our luxury suite as well as the balance of our vacation.

One final note: I reminded my daughter, Sara, about this success story and, in light of it, asked if she might consider raising my anger management grade from a B. "No way, Dad!" she insisted. Hopefully, I will refine some of my techniques and become a better practitioner in time for the next edition of this book.

References

Conger, R., K. Kim, et al. 2003. "Angry and aggressive behavior across three generations: A prospective, longitudinal study of parents and children." *Journal of Abnormal Child Psychology* 31: 143–60.

Gladwell, M. 2005. *Blink.* New York: Little, Brown and Company.

Johnson, P. L., and K. D. O'Leary. 1987. "Parental behavior patterns and conduct disorders in girls." *Journal of Abnormal Child Psychology* 15: 573–81.

Matthews, K. A., K. L. Woodall, K. Kenyon, and T. Jacob. 1996. "Negative family environment as a predictor of boys' future status on measures of hostile attitudes." *Health Psychology* 15: 30–37.

Peck, M. S. 1978. *The Road Less Traveled.* New York: Touchstone Books.

Tavris, C. 1989. *Anger: The Misunderstood Emotion.* New York: Touchstone Books.

Wallerstein, J., J. Lewis, and S. Blakeslee. 2000. *The Unexpected Legacy of Divorce: A Twenty-Five-Year Landmark Study.* New York: Hyperion.

Weidner, G., T. Rice, S. S. Knox, et al. 2000. "Familial resemblance for hostility: The National Heart, Lung and Blood Institute Family Heart Study." *Psychosomatic Medicine* 62: 197–204.

Suggested Reading

Barefoot, J. C., W. G. Dahlstrom, and R. B. Williams. 1984. "Hostility, CHD incidence, and total mortality: A 25-year follow-up study of 255 physicians." *Psychosomatic Medicine* 45: 59–63.

Chesney, M. A., and R. H. Rosenman. 1985. *Anger and Hostility in Cardiovascular Disorders.* New York: McGraw-Hill International.

Eng, P. M., G. Fitzmaurice, L. D. Kubzansky, et al. 2003. "Anger expression and risk of stroke and coronary heart disease among male health professionals." *Psychosomatic Medicine* 65: 100–10.

Friedman, M., and R. H. Rosenman. 1974. *Type A Behavior and Your Heart.* New York: Knopf.

Friedman, M., C. E. Thoresen, et al. 1986. "Alteration of Type-A behavior and its effect on cardiac recurrences in post–myocardial infarction patients: summary results of the Recurrent Coronary Prevention Project." *American Heart Journal* 112: 653–65.

Friedman, M., and D. Ulmer. 1984. *Treating Type A Behavior and Your Heart.* New York: Knopf.

Hanh, T. N. 2001. *Anger.* New York: Riverhead Books.

Lerner, H. 1986. *The Dance of Anger.* New York: Harper & Row.

Lorenz, K. 1966. *On Aggression.* Translated by Marjorie Kerr Wilson. New York: Harcourt, Brace & World.

Miller, T. Q., T. W. Smith, C. W. Turner, et al. 1996. "A meta-analytic review of research on hostility and health." *Psychological Bulletin* 119: 322–48.

Mittleman, M. A., M. Maclure, J. B. Sherwood, et al. 1995. "For the determinants of myocardial infarction onset study investigators. Triggering of acute myocardial infarction onset by episodes of anger." *Circulation* 92: 1720–25.

Nay, W. R. 2004. *Taking Charge of Anger: How to resolve conflict, sustain relationships, and express yourself without losing control.* New York: Guilford Press.

Roffman, A. E. 2004. "Is anger a thing-to-be-managed?" *Psychotherapy: Theory, Research, Practice, Training* 41: 161–71.

Williams, J. E., F. J. Nieto, C. O. Sanford, et al. 2002. "The association between trait anger and incident stroke risk: The Atherosclerosis Risk in Communities (ARIC) study." *Stroke* 33: 13–20.

Williams, J. E., C. C. Paton, I. C. Siegler, et al. 2000. "Anger proneness predicts coronary heart disease risk: Prospective analysis from the Atherosclerosis Risk in Communities (ARIC) study." *Circulation* 101: 2034–39.

Williams, R., and V. Williams. 1993. *Anger Kills*. New York: Harper Collins.

By the Author

Allan, R., and S. Scheidt, eds. 1996. *Heart & Mind: The Practice of Cardiac Psychology*. Washington, D.C.: American Psychological Association.

Allan, R., and S. Scheidt. 1998. "Group psychotherapy for cardiac patients." *International Journal of Group Psychotherapy* 48: 187–214.

——. 1999. "Psychosocial treatment of cardiac patients." *Clinical Trials in Cardiovascular Disease:*

A Companion to Braunwald's Heart Disease, edited by C. H. Henneckens et al. Philadelphia: W.B. Saunders & Co.

Allan, R., and S. Mittal. 2001. "Clinical case history: anger and the heart." *Cardiovascular Reviews & Reports, XXII*: 579–80.

Allan, R. 2002. *Cardiac Psychology*. American Psychological Association Psychotherapy Video Series III.

Allan, R., A. Linfante, S. C. Smith, et al. 2003. "Psychosocial factors predict coronary heart disease, but what predicts psychosocial risk in women?" *Journal of the American Medical Women's Medical Association* 58: 248–53.

Allan, R., and S. Scheidt. 2004. "Cardiac psychology: psychosocial factors." *Clinical Trials in Heart Disease: A Companion to Braunwald's Heart Disease, Second Edition*, edited by J. E. Manson et al. Philadelphia: Elsevier Saunders.

Allan, R., S. Scheidt, and C. Smith. In press. "Cardiac psychology/behavioral cardiology." *Cambridge Handbook of Psychology, Health & Medicine, Second Edition*, edited by S. Ayers, A. Baum, C. McManus, et al. New York: Cambridge University Press.

Index